Crochet Stitch Sampler

Baby Blankets

Crochet Stitch Sampler
Baby Blankets

30 Afghans to Explore New Stitches

Kristi Simpson

**STACKPOLE
BOOKS**

Guilford, Connecticut

Published by Stackpole Books
An imprint of Globe Pequot, the trade division of
The Rowman & Littlefield Publishing Group, Inc.
4501 Forbes Blvd., Ste. 200
Lanham, MD 20706
www.stackpolebooks.com

Distributed by NATIONAL BOOK NETWORK
800-462-6420

British Library Cataloguing in Publication Information available

Library of Congress Cataloging-in-Publication Data

Names: Simpson, Kristi, author.
Title: Crochet stitch sampler baby blankets : 30 afghans to explore new stitches /
  Kristi Simpson.
Description: First edition. | Guilford, Connecticut : Stackpole Books, [2021] | Includes
  index. | Summary: "Stitch sampler blankets offer a great canvas for learning new
  stitches and exploring new techniques in small portions. The variety of constructions
  of the blankets in this book keep your mind engaged and your hook flying. Each
  of the 30 patterns gives full written instructions and all the stitch details you need
  to complete each blanket confidently, even if the stitches are new to you"
  —Provided by publisher.
Identifiers: LCCN 2021017565 (print) | LCCN 2021017566 (ebook) | ISBN
  9780811738750 (paper ; alk. paper) | ISBN 9780811768771 (electronic)
Subjects: LCSH: Crocheting--Patterns. | Afghans (Coverlets) | Blankets.
Classification: LCC TT825 .S546275 2021 (print) | LCC TT825 (ebook) | DDC
746.43/40437--dc23
LC record available at https://lccn.loc.gov/2021017565
LC ebook record available at https://lccn.loc.gov/2021017566

∞™ The paper used in this publication meets the minimum requirements of American
National Standard for Information Sciences—Permanence of Paper for Printed Library
Materials, ANSI/NISO Z39.48-1992.

First Edition

Contents

Introduction

Whether you picked up this book because you want to make a baby blanket for a gift or for your own sweet little one, my hope is that you are inspired by the colorful yarn and cute photos to discover ways to make your blanket uniquely yours.

Each blanket has a variety of stitches to keep your mind interested in the project. Each row or section is fresh, new, and different. When I make blankets, I need them to be interesting or I get bored. I enjoyed crocheting these blankets, and mixing stitches makes them fun to finish! Some of the patterns are more extensive, but that does not mean they are difficult. Pick a pattern, personalize the colors, and have fun learning new stitches!

Speaking of stitches, there's a huge variety. It's in the title: Stitch Sampler! Stitches in this book range from bobble, criss-cross, cable, post stitches, puff, moss, filet, shells, box stitch, clusters, diamonds, treble shell, star stitch, and MORE!

Now, let's talk about the yarn. I love working with a variety of colors and textures! You can use the same colors and brands as I do, or you can substitute the same weight. Change the colors and personalize your blanket, too! These blankets are a great way to use up your scrap yarn! Dig it out and use it up. Another idea is to use self-striping, or variegated, yarns. These yarns do all of the color work for you, and you don't have to manually change the colors.

In closing, let me leave you with the best tip that is worth its weight in gold: weave in the loose ends as you go! Okay, call me silly, but if you don't, you'll have a shaggy rug instead of a blanket, and the task of weaving them in at the end will seem daunting. So, say no to shaggy rugs and weave in those ends!

Now, grab your hook and favorite yarn and create a beautiful stitch sampler blanket of your own.

—Kristi Simpson

Sweet Pea Blanket

This stitch sampler is made using one color but it brings a wow factor with texture!

Yarn
Bernat Maker Home Dec; bulky weight #5; 72% acrylic/28% nylon; 8.8 oz (250 g)/317 yds (290 m) per skein
2 skeins: Green Pea

Hooks and Other Materials
US size M-13 (9 mm) crochet hook
Yarn needle

Finished Measurements
24 in. (61 cm) wide and 34 in. (86.5 cm) long

Gauge
12 sts x 4 rows = 4 in. (10 cm) in dc

Special Stitches
Hdc in back horizontal bar: Locate the *top* loops you normally crochet into. On the WS (or back side) of the hdc, you'll see a horizontal bar. Work your hdc into this bar. (See photo tutorial in Stitch Guide on page 138.)

Pattern Notes
- The beginning ch 2 will not count as a st.
- The beginning ch 3 counts as the first dc.
- The beginning ch 6 counts as the first dc plus ch 3.
- For photo tutorial on working into the back loop only (blo), see Stitch Guide on page 136.

INSTRUCTIONS

Ch 51.

Row 1 (RS): Sc in 2nd ch from hook and in each ch across, turn. (50 sc)

Row 2: Ch 1, sc in each st across, turn.

Row 3: Ch 3, *sk 1 st, dc 2, working in FRONT of 2 dc, dc in skipped st; rep from * to last st, dc in last st, turn.

Row 4: Ch 3, turn; *sk 1 st, dc 2, working BEHIND completed 2 dc, dc in skipped st; rep from * to last st, dc in last st, turn.

Rows 5–10: Rep Rows 3 and 4.

Rows 11 and 12: Ch 1, sc in each st across, turn.

Row 13: Ch 2, hdc in each st across, turn.

Row 14: Ch 2, hdc in back horizontal bar of each hdc across, turn.

Row 15: Ch 2, working in back loop only (blo), hdc in each st across, turn.

Row 16: Rep Row 14.

Row 17: Ch 1, working in the blo, sc in each st across, turn.

Row 18: Ch 1, sc in each st across, turn.

Rows 19–30: Rep Rows 3 and 4.

Rows 31–36: Rep Rows 13–18.

Rows 37–48: Rep Rows 3 and 4. Do not fasten off.

Border

Rnd 1 (RS): Ch 3, dc in each st across top, (dc, ch 3, dc) in last st, turn to work along side edge, dc evenly across to last st, work (dc, ch 3, dc) in first st of Row 1, dc in each st across, work (dc, ch 3, dc) in last st, turn to work along side edge, dc in each st across, work (dc, ch 3) in first st; join with a sl st to beg ch 3.

Rnd 2: Sl st to ch-3 sp, (ch 6, dc) in same sp, *ch 4, sk 1 st, sl st to next st; rep from * to next ch-3 sp, (dc, ch 3, dc) in corner ch-3 sp; rep from * around; join with a sl st to 3rd ch of beg ch 6.

Rnd 3: Sl st to ch-3 sp, (ch 6, dc) in same sp, *ch 4, sl st to next ch-4 sp; rep from * to next ch-3 sp, (dc, ch 3, dc) in corner ch-3 sp; rep from * around, join with a sl st to 3rd ch of beg ch 6. Fasten off.

Finishing

Weave in ends.

Woven Love Stroller Blanket

Raid your yarn stash and work up this textured beauty. Sometimes working with just a few stitches has a big impact. Repeating a set of stitches can make a huge difference!

Yarn

Premier Anti-Pilling Worsted; medium weight #4; 100% acrylic; 3.5 oz (100 g)/180 yds (165 m) per skein

1 skein each: 100-16 Kiwi (**A**), 100-23 Mist (**B**), 100-26 Grenadine (**C**), 100-06 Baby Pink (**D**), 100-43 Wild Blue (**E**)

Hooks and Other Materials

US size J-10 (6 mm) crochet hook
Yarn needle

Finished Measurements

22 in. (56 cm) wide and 25 in. (63.5 cm) long

Gauge

12 dc x 8 rows = 4 in. (10 cm)

Special Stitches

Back post treble crochet (BPtr): Yo twice, insert hook from back to front then to back, going around post of indicated st, draw up a lp, (yo and draw through 2 lps on hook) 3 times. Skip st in front of the BPtr. (See photo tutorial in Stitch Guide on page 147.)

Front post treble crochet (FPtr): Yo twice, insert hook from front to back then to front, going around post of indicated st, draw up a lp, (yo and draw through 2 lps on hook) 3 times. Skip st behind the FPtr. (See photo tutorial in Stitch Guide on page 146.)

Hdc in back horizontal bar: Locate the *top* loops you normally crochet into. On the WS (or back side) of the hdc, you'll see a horizontal bar. Work your hdc into this bar. (See photo tutorial in Stitch Guide on page 138.)

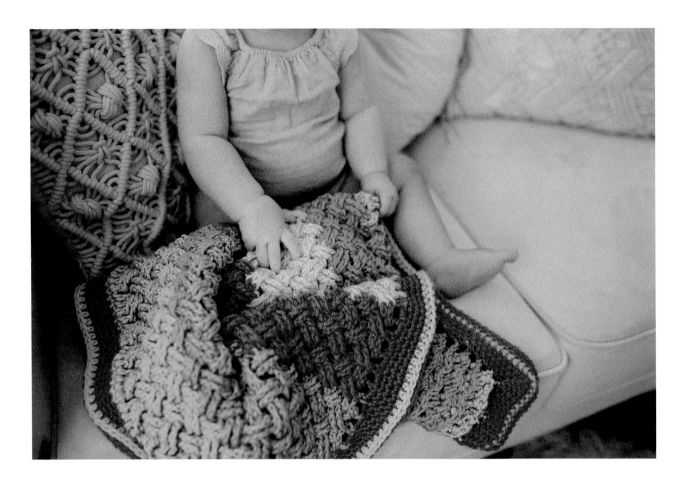

Pattern Notes
- The beginning ch 3 counts as the first dc.
- To change yarn color, work last st of old color to last yarn over. Yarn over with new color and draw through all loops on hook to complete st. Fasten off old color. Proceed with new color. (See photo tutorial in Stitch Guide on page 133.)

INSTRUCTIONS
With A, ch 71.

Row 1 (RS): Sc in the 2nd ch from hook and in each ch across, turn. (70 sts)

Row 2: Ch 3, dc in each st across, turn.

Row 3: Ch 3, *sk 2 sts, FPtr in next 2 sts, FPtr in the first skipped st, FPtr in the second skipped st; rep from * to last st, dc in last st, turn.

Row 4: Ch 3, BPtr in next 2 sts, *sk 2 sts, BPtr in next 2 sts, BPtr in the first skipped st, BPtr in the second skipped st; rep from * to last 3 stitches, BPtr 2 in next 2 sts, dc in last st, turn.

Rows 5 and 6: Rep Rows 3 and 4.

Rep Rows 3 and 4 three times per color in order B, C, D, E, for a total of 6 rows each.

With A, rep Rows 3 and 4 one time. Fasten off.

Weave in ends.

Border
Rnd 1: With RS facing, join C in last st of last row. Ch 1, turn to work along side edge, sc evenly along side edge to next corner, work 3 sc in first sc of Row 1, sc evenly across to last st, work 3 sc in last st, sc evenly along remaining edge, work 3 sc in first sc of last row, sc evenly across top edge to last st, work 3 sc in last st; join with sl st to first st.

Rnds 2–4: Ch 1, sc in each st with 3 sc in each corner; join with sl st to first sc.

Join D.

Rnd 5: Ch 2, hdc in each st around with 3 hdc in each corner; join with sl st to first hdc.

Join C.

Rnd 6: Ch 1, sc in back horizontal bar of each hdc around with 3 dc in each corner; join with sl st to first sc.

Fasten off.

Finishing
Weave in ends.

Franklin Drake Blanket

When I need a blanket for a gift and I need one fast, my go-to is a variegated super bulky weight #6 yarn. Mixing the bulky yarn with open stitches and texture you have a gift-worthy blanket!

Yarn

Lion Brand Yarn Mandala Thick & Quick; super bulky weight #6; 100% acrylic; 5.3 oz (150 g)/87 yds (79 m) per skein
6 skeins: 528-203 Stairwell

Hooks and Other Materials

US size M-13 (9 mm) crochet hook
Yarn needle

Finished Measurements

32 in. (81 cm) wide and 30 in. (76 cm) long

Gauge

8 dc x 4 rows = 4 in. (10 cm)

Special Stitches

Cluster (cl): *Yo, insert hook in specified sp and draw up a lp to height of a dc, yo, and draw through 2 lps; rep from * twice in same sp, yo and draw through 4 lps.
Shell: In specified sp, work (tr, ch 4, cl).

Pattern Notes

- The beginning ch 3 counts as the first dc.
- The beginning ch 5 counts as the first dc plus ch 2.

INSTRUCTIONS

Ch 59.

Row 1 (RS): Dc in 5th ch from hook, *ch 2, sk 2 chs, dc in next ch; rep from * across, turn.

Row 2: Ch 3, sk first ch-2 sp, *shell in next ch-2 sp, sk next ch-2 sp; rep from * across to last ch-2 sp, shell in last sp, dc in 3rd ch of turning ch, turn. (9 shells and 2 dc)

Row 3: Ch 3, *dc in top of first cl, ch 2, dc in 3rd ch of next ch-4 sp; rep from * across, ending last rep with ch 2, dc in top of turning ch, turn.

Row 4: Ch 3, *2 dc in next ch-2 sp, dc in next dc; rep from * across ending with a dc in top of turning ch, turn. (57 dc)

Row 5: Ch 1, sl st in each st across, turn.

Row 6: Ch 3, dc in each dc from Row 4 across, turn.

Row 7: Ch 3, dc in next st, *ch 2, sk 2 dc, dc in next st, rep from * across, turn.

Row 8: Ch 3, *shell in next ch-2 sp, sk next ch-2 sp; rep from * across to last ch-2 sp, shell in last sp, dc in 3rd ch of turning ch, turn. (9 shells and 2 dc)

Row 9: Rep Row 3.

Rows 10–12: Rep Rows 4–6.

Rows 13–44: Rep Rows 5 and 6.

Row 45: Rep Row 7, turn.

Border

Rnd 1 (WS): Ch 5, dc in same st, *2 dc in next ch-2 sp, dc in next dc; rep from * across ending with a (dc, ch 2, dc) in top of turning ch, turn to work along side edge, dc evenly along side edge to next corner** to Row 1, (dc, ch 2, dc) in first dc, rep from *, ending rep at **; join with sl st to 3rd ch of beg ch 5.

Finishing

Weave in ends.

Candy Lane Blankie

Are you new to crochet? Have you ventured into new stitches? This blanket is a great way to practice a few interesting stitches, and the wide stripes make a pretty statement!

Yarn
Premier Anti-Pilling Worsted; medium weight #4; 100% acrylic; 3.5 oz (100 g)/180 yds (165 m) per skein
1 skein each: 100-10 Aubergine (**A**), 100-32 Peony (**B**), 100-31 Peacock (**C**), 100-28 Mustard (**D**), 100-23 Mist (**E**), 100-30 Glass (**F**)

Hooks and Other Materials
US size J-10 (6 mm) crochet hook
Yarn needle

Finished Measurements
28 in. (71 cm) wide and 48 in. (122 cm) long

Gauge
14 sts x 16 rows = 4 in. (10 cm) in sc

Special Stitches
3-dc puff: (Yo, insert hook in next st, yo, draw yarn through st, yo, draw yarn through 2 lps on hook) 3 times in same st, yo, draw yarn through 4 lps on hook.

Pattern Notes
- The beginning ch 3 counts as the first dc.
- The beginning ch 4 counts as the first dc plus ch 1.
- To change yarn color, work last st of old color to last yarn over. Yarn over with new color and draw through all loops on hook to complete st. Fasten off old color. Proceed with new color. (See photo tutorial in Stitch Guide on page 133.)

INSTRUCTIONS

With A, ch 84.

Row 1 (RS): Sc in second ch from hook and in each ch across, turn. (83 sc)

Row 2: Ch 3, dc in same st as ch, sk 1 sc, *2 dc in next sc, sk 1 sc; rep from * across to last sc, dc in last sc, turn.

Change to B.

Row 3: Ch 1, sc in each st across, turn.

Row 4: Ch 3, *sk 1 st, 2 dc in next st; rep from * across, turn.

Row 5: Ch 1, 2 sc in first st, sk 1 st, *2 sc in next st, sk 1 st; rep from * across, ending with sc in last st, turn.

Change to C.

Row 6: Ch 3, 2 dc in same st as ch, sk 3 sts, *sc in next sc, ch 3, 3 dc in last sc made, sk next 3 sc; rep from * across to last 2 sts, sk 1, sc in last st, turn.

Row 7: Ch 3, 2 dc in same st as ch, (sc, ch 3, 3 dc) in each ch-3 sp across to turning ch, sc in 3rd ch of turning ch, turn.

Row 8: Ch 1, sc in first sc, ch 3, dc in last sc made, *sc in top of next ch-3 sp, ch 3, dc in last sc made, rep from * across to last ch-3 sp, sk next 3 sts, sc in 3rd ch of turning ch, turn.

Change to D.

Row 9: Ch 4, dc in next ch-3 sp, ch 1, *dc in next sc, ch 1, dc in next ch-3 sp, ch 1; rep from * across to last sc, dc in last sc, turn. (85 sts)

Row 10: Ch 1, sc in first dc, sc2tog, *sc in the next ch, sc in next dc; rep from * across to last 3 sts, sc2tog, sc in turning ch, turn. (83 sc)

Change to E.

Row 11: Ch 1, sc in each st across, turn.

Change to B.

Row 12: Ch 3 (counts as dc), 3-dc puff st in next sc, *ch 1, sk next sc, 3-dc puff in next sc; rep from * across to last sc, dc in last st, turn.

Change to E.

Row 13: Ch 1, sc in each st and ch across, turn.

Change to A.

Rows 14–23: Rep Rows 4–13.

Change to E.

Rows 24–33: Rep Rows 4–13.

Change to C.

Rows 34–43: Rep Rows 4–13.

Change to D.

Rows 44–53: Rep Rows 4–13.

Change to B.

Rows 54–63: Rep Rows 4–13.

Change to F.

Rows 64–73: Rep Rows 4–13.

Change to E.

Row 74: Rep Row 13.

Change to B.

Row 75: Rep Row 12.

Change to E.

Row 76: Rep Row 11.

Change to D.

Row 77: Rep Row 10.

Row 78: Ch 4 (counts as dc and ch 1), sk next sc, dc in next ch-3 sp, ch 1, *dc in next sc, ch 1, dc in next ch-3 sp, ch 1; rep from * across to last sc, dc in last sc, turn.

Change to C.

Row 79: Ch 1, turn, sc in first sc, ch 3, dc in last sc made, *sk next 3 sts, ch 3, dc in last sc made; rep from *, sc in 3rd ch of turning ch.

Row 80: Ch 3, 2 dc in same st as ch, (sc, ch 3, 3 dc) in each ch-3 sp across to turning ch, sc in 3rd ch of turning ch, turn.
Change to F.

Row 81: Rep Row 5.

Row 82: Rep Row 4.

Row 83: Ch 1, sc in each st and sp across, turn. Change to A.

Row 84: Rep Row 2.

Row 85: Ch 1, sc in each st across. Fasten off.

Finishing
Weave in ends.

Sunny Days Blanket

Tummy time has never been more fun! The details and stitches make this blanket the perfect baby shower gift, and the circular shape makes it even more unique.

Yarn

Bernat Maker Home Dec; bulky weight #5; 72% acrylic/28% nylon; 8.8 oz (250 g)/317 yds (290 m) per skein
1 skein each: 11003 Gold (**A**), 11013 Sunset Sea (**B**), 11005 Aqua (**C**)

Hooks and Other Materials

US size M-13 (9 mm) crochet hook
Yarn needle

Finished Measurements

About 32 in. (81 cm) diameter

Gauge

12 sc x 10 rows = 4 in. (10 cm) in sc

Special Stitches

2-dc cluster (2-dc cl): *Yo, insert hook in specified sp and draw up a lp to height of a dc, yo, and draw through 2 lps; rep from * in same sp, yo and draw through 3 lps.
Cluster (cl): *Yo, insert hook in specified sp and draw up a lp to height of a dc, yo, and draw through 2 lps; rep from * twice in same sp, yo and draw through 4 lps.
Shell: [Tr, (ch 1, tr) 6 times] in the same specified sp.

Pattern Notes

• The beginning ch 2 will not count as a st.
• To change yarn color, work last st of old color to last yarn over. Yarn over with new color and draw through all loops on hook to complete st.

Rnd 5: Ch 1, *sc in next 3 sts, 2 sc in next st, rep from * around; join with sl st to first sc. (100 sts)
Change to A.

Rnd 6: Ch 2, 2-dc cl in same st as beg ch 2, ch 2, sk 2 sts, cl, ch 2, sk 1 st, *cl, ch 2, sk 2 sts, cl, ch 2, sk 1 st; rep from * around; join with sl st to first 2-dc cl. (120 sts)
Change to B.

Rnd 7: Ch 2, dc in same st as beg ch 2, *2 dc in next ch-sp, dc in next st, 3 dc in next ch-sp**, dc in next st; rep from * around, ending last rep at **; join with sl st to first dc. (140 sts)
Change to C.

Rnd 8: Ch 2, dc in same st as beg ch 2, ch 2, 2-dc cl in same st, sk 3 sts, (2-dc cl, ch 2, 2-dc cl) in next st, sk 2 sts, *(2-dc cl, ch 2, 2-dc cl) in next st, sk 3 sts, (2-dc cl, ch 2, 2-dc cl in next st, sk 2 sts; rep from * around; join with sl st to first dc. (160 sts)
Change to A.

Rnd 9: Ch 1, *(sc, ch 1, sc, ch 1, sc) in first ch-2 sp, ch 1, (sc, ch 1, sc) in next ch-2 sp; rep from * around; join with sl st to first sc. (180 sts)
Change to B.

Fasten off old color. Proceed with new color. (See photo tutorial in Stitch Guide on page 133.)
- For photo tutorial on working around the post of a stitch, see Stitch Guide on page 144.

INSTRUCTIONS

With A, ch 7, sl st to the first chain to join.

Rnd 1: Ch 2, 20 dc in ring; join with a sl st to first dc. (20 dc)

Rnd 2: Ch 2, 2 dc in same st as beg ch 2, 2 dc in each remaining st around; join with sl st to first dc. (40 dc)

Rnd 3: Ch 2, 2-dc cl in same st as beg ch 2, ch 2, sk 1 st, *cl, ch 2, sk 1 st; rep from * around; join with sl st to first 2-dc cl. (60 sts)
Change to B.

Rnd 4: Ch 2, dc in same st as beg ch 2, 3 dc in ch-2 space, *dc in next st, 3 dc in next ch-2 sp; rep from * around; join with sl st to first dc. (80 sts)
Change to C.

Rnd 10: Ch 2, (dc, dc on post of last dc made) in the same st as beg ch 2, sk ch-1 sp, *(dc, dc on post of last dc made) in next sc, sk ch-1 sp; rep from * around; join with sl st to first dc. (200 sts)
Change to C.

Rnd 11: Ch 1, *sc in next 9 sts, 2 sc in the next st; rep from * around; join with sl st to first sc. (220 sts)
Change to A.

Rnd 12: Ch 2, 2-dc cl in same st as beg ch 2, ch 2, sk 2 sts, cl, ch 2, sk 2 sts, cl, ch 2, sk 2 sts, cl, ch 2, sk 1 st, *(cl, ch 2, sk 2 sts) 3 times, cl, ch 2, sk 1 st; rep from * around; join with sl st to first ch-2 cl. (240 sts)
Change to B.

Rnd 13: Ch 2, *2 dc in next cl, 2 dc in next ch-sp, (dc in cl, 2 dc in next ch-sp) 3 times; rep from * around; join with sl st to to first dc. (260 sts)
Change to C.

Rnd 14: Ch 2, ch 1, 2 dc in same st as beg ch 2, ch 1, 2 dc in next st in same st, sk 2 sts, [(2-dc cl, ch 1, 2-dc cl), sk 2 sts] 3 times, (2-dc cl, ch 2, 2-dc cl), sk 1 st, *[(2-dc cl, ch 1, 2-dc cl)] sk 2 sts, [(2-dc cl, ch 2, 2-dc cl), sk 1 st] twice; rep from * around; join with sl st to first dc. (328 sts) Fasten off.

Rnd 15: Join A in ch-1 sp, ch 1, 2 sc in each ch-2 space; join with sl st to first sc. (328 sts)
Change to B.

Rnd 16: Ch 2, dc in same st as beg ch 2, dc in each st around; join with sl st to first dc. (328 sts)

Rnd 17: Ch 1, *sc in next st, sk 3 sts, shell in next st, sk 3 sts; rep from * around; join with sl st to first sc. (41 shells, 41 sc) Fasten off.

Finishing
Weave in ends.

Baby Delight

Texture, color, and multiple stitch patterns work together to create this whimsical baby blanket. This is a great pattern for using up scraps or for coordinating your colors with the nursery's decor.

Yarn
Caron Simply Soft; medium weight #4; 100% acrylic; 6 oz (170 g)/171 yds (156 m) per skein

1 skein each: Fuchsia (**A**), Strawberry (**B**), Persimmon (**C**), Sunshine (**D**), Chartreuse (**E**), Cobalt (**F**), Violet (**G**), Orchid (**H**), Off White (**I**)

Hooks and Other Materials
US size J-10 (6 mm) crochet hook
Yarn needle

Finished Measurements
30 in. (76 cm) wide and 50 in. (127 cm) long

Gauge
12 sts x 12 rows = 4 in. (10 cm) in sc

Special Stitches
Star Stitch:

First star: Ch 3, turn; insert hook into the 2nd ch from the hook and pull up a lp. Then do the same in the 3rd ch and then the base st; insert hook into the next st, pull up a lp. This leaves you with 5 lps on the hook. Do not pull loops tight, keep loose. Yo and pull through all 5 lps. Ch 1 to finish off the st. First star made.

Each star to end of row: Insert the hook into the ch 1 just made, and pull up a lp. Insert the hook into the same st that the last star st was in, yo and pull up a lp. Keep all lps on hook. Insert hook into the next st, yo and pull up lp. Insert hook into next st and pull up lp. This leaves you with 5 lps on hook, do not pull tight. Yo, pull through all lps, ch 1 to finish the st.

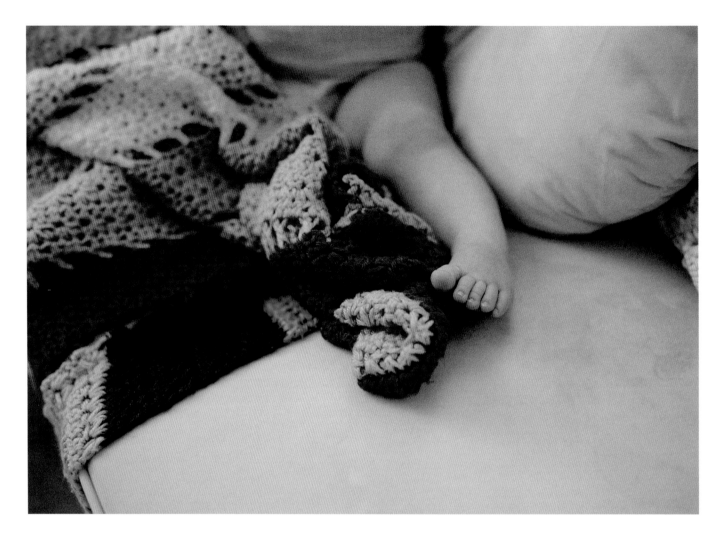

Pattern Notes
- The beginning ch 2 will not count as a stitch.
- The beginning ch 5 will count as dc plus ch 2.
- To change yarn color, work last st of old color to last yarn over. Yarn over with new color and draw through all loops on hook to complete st. Fasten off old color. Proceed with new color. (See photo tutorial in Stitch Guide on page 133.)
- The Short Rows will be made in short back and forth rows in one long panel for the top. The Long Rows will be made on one edge of the Short Rows to complete the blanket.

INSTRUCTIONS
First Column: Short Rows
With A, ch 16.

Row 1 (RS): Sc in the 2nd ch from hook and in each ch across, turn. (15 sts)

Row 2: Star Stitch (see Special Stitches) across, turn.

Row 3: Ch 2, hdc in each st and ch-1 sp across, turn.

Rows 4–9: Rep Rows 2 and 3. Join next color.

Rows 10–81: Rep Rows 2–9 using each color in the following order: B, C, D, E, F, G, H, I, A.

Row 82: Ch 2, hdc in each st across.Fasten off.

Long Rows
Row 1: With A, join in corner of RS of First Column, ch 5 (counts as first dc and ch 2), working in ends of rows as sts, sk 2 sts, dc in the next st, *ch 2, sk 2 sts; rep from * to end of row; dc in end of hdc row. (28 dc, 27 ch-2 sps).

Row 2: Ch 2, hdc in each st and 2 hdc in each ch-2 sp across, turn. (82 sts)

Row 3: Star Stitch across, turn.

Row 4: Ch 2, hdc in each st and ch-1 sp across, turn.

Rows 5 and 6: Rep Rows 3 and 4.

Row 7: Join B (or next color), ch 5, sk 2 sts, dc in next st, *ch 2, sk 2 sts, dc in next st, rep from * to end.

Row 8: Ch 2, hdc in each st and ch-1 sp across, turn.

Row 9: Star Stitch across, turn.

Row 10: Ch 2, hdc in each st and ch-1 sp across, turn.

Rows 11 and 12: Rep Rows 9 and 10.
Rep Rows 7–12, using each color in the following
order: C, D, E, F, G, H, I, A.
Fasten off.

Finishing
Weave in ends.

Cocoa Strips

Made in small strips, this is a great on-the-go project. You'll be working with shell stitch and a double crochet set, and it's fun to watch this blanket come together! Pick out your colors and get started right away!

Yarn

Red Heart Soft; medium weight #4; 100% acrylic; 5 oz (141 g)/256 yds (234 m) per skein
1 skein each: E728-4601 Off White (**A**), E728-9274 Biscuit (**B**), E728-1882 Toast (**C**)

Hooks and Other Materials

US size H-8 (5 mm) crochet hook
Yarn needle

Finished Measurements

37 in. (95 cm) wide and 25½ in. (65 cm) long

Gauge

7 rows = 4 in. (10 cm) in pattern Rows 1–7

Pattern Notes

- The beginning ch 3 counts as the first dc.
- The beginning ch 4 counts as the first dc plus ch 1.

INSTRUCTIONS

Strip

Make 5 in A, 4 in B, 4 in C.

Ch 8.

Row 1 (RS): Dc in 6th ch from hook (counts as dc and ch 1), ch 1, sk 1, dc in next ch, turn. (3 dc and 2 ch-1 sps)

Row 2: Ch 3, sk 1 ch, 5 dc in next dc, sk 1 ch, dc in last dc, turn. (7 dc)

Row 3: Ch 4, sk 2 dc, dc in next dc, ch 1, sk 2 dc, dc in last dc, turn. (3 dc and 2 ch-1 sps)

Rows 4–47: Rep Rows 2 and 3. Do not turn at end of Row 47.

Border

Rnd 1: Ch 3, turn to work along long side edge, 2 dc in end of each row, 10 dc in middle dc of Row 1, turn to work along long side edge, 2 dc in end of each row, 10 dc in middle dc of Row 47; join with sl st to beg ch 3. Fasten off.

Assembly

Use yarn needle to sew strips together along long side edges.

Finishing

Weave in ends.

Cupcake Squares Blanket

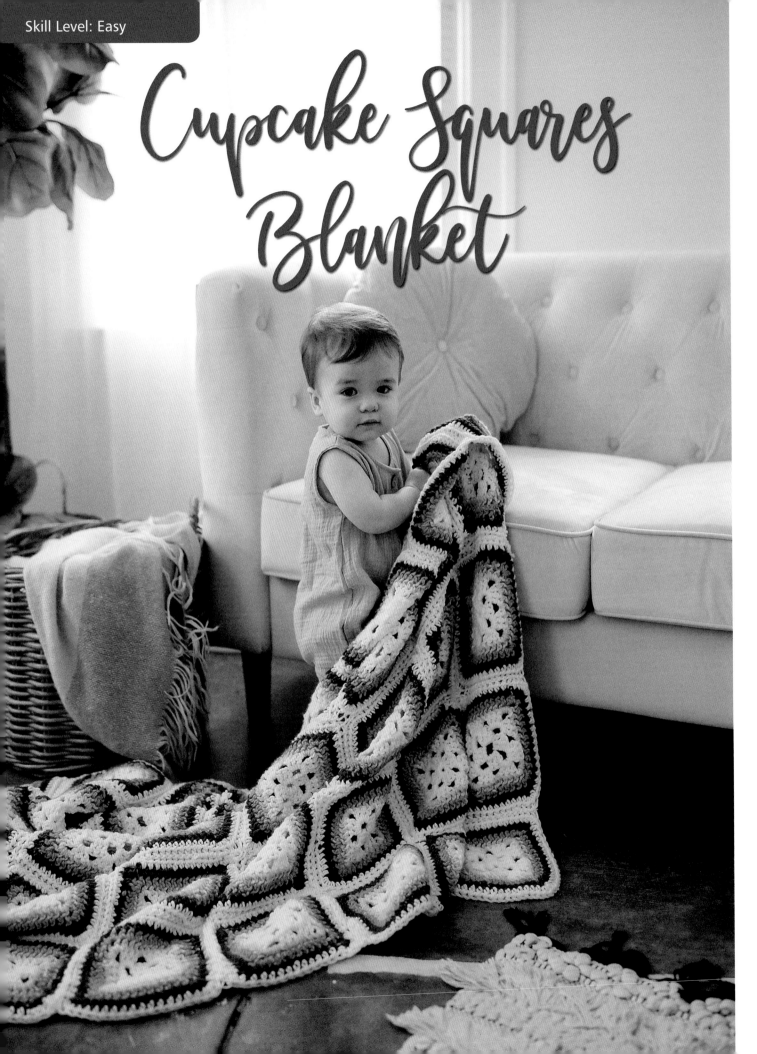

This block blanket is made with 6-inch squares. Stitches include double crochet and half double crochet, and you will learn how to work in the back horizontal bar of the half double crochet. Mix and match colors and create a unique blanket for your little cupcake!

Yarn
Lion Brand Yarn Vanna's Choice; medium weight #4; 100% acrylic; 3.5 oz (100 g)/170 yds (156 m) per skein

3 skeins each: E860-100 White (**A**), E860-150 Pale Grey (**B**), E860-111 Sky Blue (**C**), E860-151 Charcoal Grey (**D**)

Hooks and Other Materials
US size J-10 (6 mm) crochet hook
Yarn needle

Finished Measurements
30 in. (76 cm) wide and 48 in. (122 cm) long

Gauge
6 in. (15 cm) per square

Special Stitches
Hdc in back horizontal bar: Locate the *top* loops you normally crochet into. On the WS (or back side) of the hdc, you'll see a horizontal bar. Work your hdc into this bar. (See photo tutorial in Stitch Guide on page 138.)

Pattern Notes
- The beginning ch 3 counts as the first dc.
- The beginning ch 2 will not count as a st.

INSTRUCTIONS

Square
Make 40.

With A, ch 4. Join in a ring.

Rnd 1: Ch 3, 2 dc in ring, ch 3, [3 dc in ring, ch 3] 3 times; join with sl st to beg ch-3. (12 dc, 4 ch-3 sp)

Rnd 2: Sl st in next 2 dc, slip st in ch-3 sp, (ch 3, 2 dc, ch 3, 3 dc) in same sp, ch 1, [(3 dc, ch 3, 3 dc) in next ch-3 sp, ch 1] 3 more times; join with sl st to beg ch 3. Fasten off. (24 dc, 4 ch-1 sp, 4 ch-3 sps)

Rnd 3: Join B in ch-3 sp, ch 2, *3 hdc in ch-3 sp, hdc in next 3 dc, hdc in ch-1 sp, hdc in next 3 dc; rep from * around; join with sl st to first hdc. Fasten off. (40 hdc)

Rnd 4: Join C in 2nd st of corner in the back horizontal bar of hdc, ch 2, working in back horizontal bar around, 3 hdc in same st, hdc in next 9 sts, *3 hdc in next st, hdc in next 9 sts; rep from * around; join with sl st to first hdc. Fasten off. (48 hdc)

Rnd 5: Join D in 2nd st of corner in the back horizontal bar of hdc, ch 2, working in back horizontal bar around, 3 hdc in same st, hdc in next 11 sts, *3 hdc in next st, hdc in next 11 sts; rep from * around; join with sl st to first hdc. Fasten off. (56 hdc)

Rnd 6: Join A in 2nd st of corner in the back horizontal bar of hdc, ch 2 (not a st), working in back horizontal bar around, 3 hdc in same st, hdc in next 13 sts, *3 hdc in next st, hdc in next 13 sts; rep from * around; join with sl st to first hdc. Fasten off. (64 hdc)

Assembly
Thread yarn needle with A and sew squares together: 5 squares across and 8 squares down.

Finishing
Weave in ends.

Canterbury Bells

This blanket is a delight. Simply let a self-striping yarn do the work for you! There are so many options available, and each will look different each time with this pattern.

Yarn
Willow Yarns Cairo Cotton; medium weight #4; 60% cotton/40% acrylic; 5.5 oz (130 g)/311 yds (284 m) per skein
3 skeins: Canterbury Bells

Hooks and Other Materials
US size I-9 (5.5 mm) crochet hook
Yarn needle

Finished Measurements
34 in. (86.5 cm) wide and 42 in. (106.5 cm) long

Gauge
4 rows = 4 in. (10 cm) in dc

Special Stitches
X-Stitch (X-st): Yo twice, insert hook in next st, yo, draw yarn through st, yo, draw yarn through 2 lps on hook (3 lps on hook), sk next st, yo, insert hook in next st, yo, draw yarn through st, (yo, draw yarn through 2 lps on hook) 4 times, ch 1, yo, insert hook through 2 strands at the center of cluster just made, yo, draw through st, (yo, draw yarn through 2 lps on hook) twice.

Pattern Notes
• The beginning ch 3 counts as the first dc.
• The beginning ch 4 counts as the first dc plus ch 1.

INSTRUCTIONS

Ch 130.

Row 1: Dc in 4th ch from hook and in next 2 chs, *ch 3, sk next 3 chs, dc in next 3 chs; rep from * across to last 4 chs, ch 3, sk next 3 chs, dc in last ch, turn. (126 sts)

Row 2: Ch 3, sk first dc, *3 dc in next ch-3 sp, ch 3; rep from * across to last ch-3 lp, dc in 3rd ch of turning ch, turn.

Rows 3–6: Rep Row 2.

Row 7: Ch 4, (dc, ch 1) in next ch-3 sp, sk 1 dc, (dc, ch 1, dc) in next dc, *(ch 1, dc, ch 1) in next ch-3 sp, sk 1 dc, (dc, ch 1, dc) in next dc, sk 1 dc, dc in 3rd ch of turning ch; rep from * across, turn.

Row 8: Ch 4, (dc, ch 1) in next ch-1 sp, (dc, ch 1, dc) in next dc, *sk 1 ch-1 sp, sk 1 dc, (ch 1, dc, ch 1) in next ch-1 sp, sk 1 dc, sk 1 ch-1 sp, (dc, ch 1, dc) in next dc; rep from * across to last st, dc in 3rd ch of turning ch, turn.

Row 9: Ch 4, (dc, ch 1) in next ch-1 sp, sk 1 dc, sk 1 ch-1 sp, (dc, ch 1, dc) in next dc, sk 1 ch-1 sp, sk 1 dc, *(ch 1, dc, ch 1) in next ch-1 sp, sk 1 dc, sk 1 ch-1 sp, (dc, ch 1, dc) in next dc; rep from * across, ending with a dc in 3rd ch of turning ch, turn.

Rows 10–13: Rep Rows 8 and 9.

Row 14: Ch 4, dc in next ch-1 sp, *ch 1, dc in next ch-1 sp; rep from * across ending with a dc in last st, turn.

Row 15: Ch 3, dc in each dc and ch-1 sp across, turn. (126 sts)

Row 16: Ch 3, dc in next dc, *ch 1, sk 1 dc, dc in next dc; rep from * across, turn.

Row 17: Rep Row 15.

Rows 18–21: Rep Rows 16 and 17.

Row 22: Ch 4, sk first st, *X-st worked across next 3 sts; rep from * across to last st, tr in last st, turn. (41 X-sts)

Row 23: Ch 1, sc in each tr and ch-1 sp across, ending with sc in 4th ch of turning ch, turn. (126 sts)

Rows 24–29: Rep Rows 22 and 23.

Row 30: Ch 3, dc in each st across, turn. (126 dc)

Row 31: Ch 3, *dc in next 3 sts, ch 3, sk 3 sts, rep from * across, ending with a dc in 3rd ch of turning ch, turn.

Rows 32–66: Rep Rows 2–31, ending on Row 6.

Border

Rnd 1: *Ch 4, sl st in 2nd ch from hook and in next 2 chs, sl st in next 2 sts; rep from * around; join with sl st to first st. Fasten off.

Finishing

Weave in ends.

Low Tide Motif Blanket

Motifs are joined as you go while using a complementary color palette that adds depth to this stunning design. No sewing together!

Yarn

Lion Brand Yarn Low Tide; medium weight #4; 81% acrylic/19% polyester; 3.5 oz (100 g)/306 yds (280 m) per skein

3 skeins each: 211-402 Cove (**A**), 211-407 Cabana (**B**), 211-400 Waves (**C**), 211-405 Coast (**D**), 211-404 Reef (**E**), 211-411 Dunes (**F**)

Hooks and Other Materials

US size 7 (4.5 mm) crochet hook
Yarn needle

Finished Measurements

36 in. (91.5 cm) wide and 36 in. (91.5 cm) long

Gauge

1 motif = 4.5 in. (11.5 cm)

Special Stitches

5-dc cluster (5-dc cl): *Yo, push hook through next st (or ch), yo and pull back through, yo and pull through first 2 lps. Keep remaining lps on hook; rep from * 4 more times, yo and pull through all 6 lps on hook to complete.

6-dc cluster (6-dc cl): *Yo, push hook through next st (or ch), yo and pull back through, yo and pull through first 2 lps. Keep remaining lps on hook; rep from * 5 more times, yo and pull through all 6 lps on hook to complete.

Pattern Notes

• The beginning ch 3 counts as the first dc.
• The beginning ch 4 counts as the first dc plus ch 1.

INSTRUCTIONS

Square 1

Ch 10, sl st to the first ch to join.

Rnd 1: Ch 3, 4 dc in ring, ch 7, *dc 5 in ring, ch 7; rep from * 2 more times; join with sl st to the beg ch-3. (20 dc, 4 ch-7 sps)

Rnd 2: Ch 4 (counts as dc and ch 1), sk 1 st, 2 dc in next st, ch 1, sk 1 st, dc in next st, ch 2, (dc, ch 1, dc, ch 5, dc, ch 1, dc) in next ch-7 sp, ch 2, *dc in next st, ch 1, sk 1 st, 2 dc in next st, ch 1, sk 1 st, dc in next st, ch 2, (dc, ch 1, dc, ch 5, dc, ch 1, dc) in ch-7 sp, ch 2; rep from * around; join with sl st to 3rd ch of beg ch 4. (32 dc, 16 ch-1 sps, 8 ch-2 sps, 5 ch-5 sps.

Rnd 3: Ch 2, 5-dc cl in same st as joining, ch 5, sl st to the first ch to create a lp, ch 4, sk 2 dc, dc in next ch-1 sp, ch 3, (2 dc, ch 3, 2 dc) in ch-5 sp, ch 3, dc in next ch-1 sp, ch 4, sk 2 dc, *6-dc cl in next dc, ch 5, sl st to the first ch to create a lp, ch 4, sk 2 dc, dc in next ch-1 sp, ch 3, (2 dc, ch 3, 2 dc) in ch-5 sp, ch 3, dc in next ch-1 sp, ch 4, sk next dc; rep from * around; join with sl st to the top of 5-dc cl. Fasten off.

All Other Squares

Ch 10, sl st to the first ch to join.

Rnd 1: Ch 3, 4 dc in ring, ch 7, *dc 5 in ring, ch 7; rep from * 2 more times; join with sl st to the beg ch 3.

Rnd 2: Ch 4, sk 1 st, 2 dc in next st, ch 1, sk 1 st, dc in next st, ch 2, (dc, ch 1, dc, ch 5, dc, ch 1, dc) in ch-7 sp, ch 2, *dc in next st, ch 1, sk 1 st, 2 dc in next st, ch 1, sk 1 st, dc in next st, ch 2, (dc, ch 1, dc, ch 5, dc, ch 1, dc) in ch-7 sp, ch 2; rep from * around; join with sl st to 3rd ch of beg ch-4.

You will join your current square to previous square(s) in Rnd 3. As you join, the pattern will be the same except when you join to the next square. Each row of the blanket will be a little different. For instance, squares on Row 1 will join on one side. The next rows will join on 2 sides. To join the last 6, there will be 2 or 3 side joins.

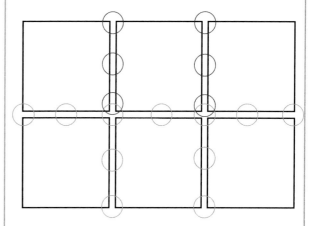

To join in *Corners:* In the ch-3 sp, 2 dc, ch 1, sl st to the next square's ch-2 (from the ch-3 corner) in the corner, ch 1, 2 dc in ch-3 space to finish corner.

To join in *Loops:* Ch 5, remove hook from the ch, slip the ch length for loop through the next square's completed loop and then sl st the working ch to the first ch-5 to join.

Chart showing motif color placement.

A	B	C	D	E	F	A	B
B	C	D	E	F	A	B	C
C	D	E	F	A	B	E	D
D	E	F	A	B	C	D	E
E	F	A	B	C	D	E	F
F	A	B	C	D	E	F	A
A	B	C	D	E	F	A	B
B	C	D	C	F	A	B	C

Rnd 3: Join as needed using above directions, ch 2 (counts as first part of cluster), 5-dc cl in same st as joining, ch 5, sl st to the first ch to create a loop, ch 4, sk 2 dc, dc in ch-1 sp, ch 3, (2 dc, ch 3, 2 dc) in ch-5 sp, ch 3, dc in ch-1 sp, ch 4, sk 2 dc, *6-dc cl starting with next dc, ch 5, sl st to the first ch to create a loop, ch 4, sk 2 dc, dc in ch-1 sp, ch 3, (2 dc, ch 3, 2 dc) in ch-5 sp, ch 3, dc in ch-1 sp, ch 4, sk dc; rep from * around; join with sl st to the top of 5-dc cl. Fasten off.

Finishing
Weave in ends.

Snuggle-Buggle Baby Blanket

This blanket has a variety of techniques included in the pattern. You'll learn new stitches and ways to add great texture in a small space!

Yarn
Lion Brand Yarn Vanna's Choice; medium weight #4; 100% acrylic; 3.5 oz (100 g)/170 yds (156 m) per skein
1 skein each: 860-150 Pale Grey (**A**), 860-098 Fisherman (**B**)
2 skeins each: 860-109 Colonial Blue (**C**), 860-130 Honey (**D**), 860-125 Taupe (**E**)

Hooks and Other Materials
US size J-10 (6 mm) crochet hook
Yarn needle

Finished Measurements
36 in. (91.5 cm) wide and 36 in. (91.5 cm) long

Gauge
13 dc and 7 rows = 4 in. (10 cm)

Special Stitches
Single crochet 2 sts together (sc2tog): (Insert hook in next st and draw up a lp) twice, yo and draw through all 3 lps on hook (1 st decreased). (See photo tutorial in Stitch Guide on page 141.)
Double crochet 2 sts together (dc2tog): (Yo, insert hook in next st and draw up a lp, yo and draw through 2 lps) twice, yo and draw through all 3 lps on hook (1 st decreased). (See photo tutorial in Stitch Guide on page 142.)
Double crochet 3 sts together (dc3tog): (Yo, insert hook in next st and draw up a lp, yo, draw through 2 lps) 3 times, yo and draw through all 4 lps on hook (2 sts decreased). (See photo tutorial in Stitch Guide on page 143.)
Cluster (cl): *Yo, insert hook in specified st and draw up a lp to height of a dc, yo and draw through 2 lps on hook; rep from * 3 times more in same st, yo and draw through 5 lps.
2-dc cluster (2-dc cl): *Yo, insert hook in specified st and draw up a lp to height of a dc, yo and draw through 2 lps on hook; rep from * 2 times more in same st, yo and draw through 3 lps: 2-dc cl complete.
Bobble: (Yo, insert hook in next st, yo, draw yarn through st and up to level of work) 4 times in same st, yo, draw yarn through 9 lps on hook.

Hdc in back horizontal bar: Locate the *top* loops you normally crochet into. On the WS (or back side) of the hdc, you'll see a horizontal bar. Work your hdc into this bar. (See photo tutorial in Stitch Guide on page 138.)

Pattern Notes
- The beginning ch 3 counts as the first dc.
- The beginning ch 4 counts as the first dc plus ch 1 unless otherwise instructed.
- The beginning ch 6 counts as the first dc plus ch 3.
- To change yarn color, work last st of old color to last yarn over. Yarn over with new color and draw through all loops on hook to complete st. Fasten off old color. Proceed with new color. (See photo tutorial in Stitch Guide on page 133.)

INSTRUCTIONS

Panels 1 and 2
Square Motif 1: Make 2.

With A, ch 22.

Row 1 (WS): Dc in 4th ch from hook and in each ch across, turn.

Row 2: Ch 1, sc in first dc, *sc in next dc, ch 4, bobble in last sc made, sk next 2 dc; rep from * across to turning ch, sc in 3rd ch of turning ch, turn.

Row 3: Ch 4 (counts as treble), 3 dc in each ch-4 sp across to last ch-4 sp, sk next sc, tr in last sc, turn.

Row 4: Ch 3, *sk next dc, dc in next 2 dc, working over last 2 dc made, dc in last skipped dc; rep from * across to turning ch, dc in 3rd ch of turning ch, turn.

Row 5: Ch 3, dc in each st across, ending with dc in 3rd ch of turning ch, turn.

Rows 6–9: Rep Rows 2–5.

Trim:

Rnd 1: Ch 1, turn, 3 sc in first st, sc in each st across top, 3 sc in last st, turn to work along side edge, sc 17 evenly across edge, work 3 sc in first st of Row 1, sc in each st across, 3 sc in last st, turn to work along side edge, sc 17 evenly across edge; join with a sl st to first sc.

Fasten off.

Square Motif 2: Make 2.

With B, ch 22.

Row 1: Dc in 4th ch from hook, dc in next ch, dc around the posts of last 2 dc made to create a wrapped st, sk next ch, *dc in each of next 2 ch, dc around the posts of last 2 dc made, sk next ch; rep from * across to last ch, dc in last ch, turn. (20 dc)

Row 2: Ch 3, dc in each dc across to turning ch, dc in 3rd ch of turning ch, turn.

Row 3: Ch 3, *dc in each of next 2 dc, dc around the posts of last 2 dc made, sk next dc; rep from * across to turning ch, dc in 3rd ch of turning ch, turn.

Rows 4–10: Rep Rows 2 and 3, ending on Row 2.

Trim:

Rnd 1: Ch 1, turn to work along side edge, sc 17 evenly across edge, 3 sc in first st of Row 1, [sc in ch-1 sp, sc in next 2 sts] 5 times, 3 sc in last st, turn to work along side edge, sc 17 evenly across edge, 3 sc in first st of Row 10, sc 20 across, 3 sc in last st; join with a sl st to first sc. Fasten off.

Square Motif 3: Make 2.

Square Motif 4: Make 2.

With C, ch 20.

Row 1: Sc in 2nd ch from hook and in each ch across, turn. (19 sc)

Row 2: Ch 1, sc in first sc; *ch 3, sk 2 sc, cl in next sc, ch 3, sk 2 sc, sc in next sc; rep from * across, turn.

Row 3: Ch 6, sc in top of first cl, *ch 3, dc in next sc, ch 3, sc in top of next cl; rep from * across, ending last rep with ch 3, dc in last sc, turn.

Row 4: Ch 1, sc in first dc, *ch 3, cl in next sc, ch 3, sc in next dc; rep from * across, ending last rep with ch 3, cl in last sc, ch 3, sc in 3rd ch of turning ch 6, turn.

Rows 5–11: Rep Rows 3 and 4, ending on Row 3.

Row 12: Ch 1, sc in first dc, *2 sc in ch-3 sp, sc in next sc, 2 sc in next ch-3 sp, sc in next dc; rep from * across, ending with dc in 3rd ch of turning ch 6.

Trim:

Rnd 1: Ch 1, turn to work along side edge, sc 17 evenly across edge, 3 sc in first st of Row 1, sc in each st across, 3 sc in last st, turn to work along side edge, sc 17 evenly across edge, 3 sc in first st of Row 12, sc in each st across, 3 sc in last st; join with a sl st to first sc. Fasten off.

With D, ch 22.

Row 1: Dc in 4th ch from hook, ch 1, dc in next ch, *sk next ch, dc in next ch, ch 1, dc in next ch; rep from * across to last 2 ch, sk next ch, dc in last ch, turn. (11 dc, 9 ch-1 sps)

Row 2: Ch 3, (dc, ch 1, dc) in each ch-1 sp across to last ch-1 sp, dc in 3rd ch of turning ch, turn.

Rows 3–10: Rep Row 2.

Trim:

Rnd 1: Ch 1, 3 sc in first st, sk 1 st, sc in each st across, 3 sc in last st, turn to work along side edge, sc 17 evenly across edge, 3 sc in first st of Row 1, sc in each st across, 3 sc in last st, turn to work along side edge, sc 17 evenly across edge; join with a sl st to first sc. Fasten off.

Square Motif 5: Make 2.

With E, ch 22.

Row 1: Dc in 4th ch from hook, sk next 2 ch, *3 dc in next ch, sk next 2 ch; rep from * across to last ch, 2 dc in last ch, turn. (19 dc)

Row 2: Ch 3, dc in next dc, ch 2, *dc3tog working across next 3 dc, ch 2; rep from * across to last 2 sts, dc2tog across last 2 sts, turn.

Row 3: Ch 3, 3 dc in each ch-2 sp across, dc in 3rd ch of turning ch, turn.

Row 4: Ch 4, dc3tog across next 3 dc, *ch 2, dc3tog worked across next 3 dc; rep from * across to turning ch, ch 1, dc in 3rd ch of turning ch, turn.

Row 5: Ch 3, dc in first dc, sk next ch-1 sp, 3 dc in each ch-2 sp across, 2 dc in 3rd ch of turning ch, turn.

Rows 6–10: Rep Rows 2–5, ending on Row 2.

Trim:

Rnd 1: Ch 1, turn, 3 sc in first dc, *2 sc in ch-2 sp, sc in next dc; rep from * across, ending with 3 sc in last dc; turn to work along side edge, sc 17 evenly across edge**, 3 sc in first st of Row 1, rep from * around, ending rep at **; join with a sl st to first sc. Fasten off.

Assembly

Make sure all RS are facing up and sew 5 squares together in 1 panel. Repeat for second panel. You will have 2 panels, one for the top and one for the bottom of the blanket.

Panel 3

Row 1: With RS facing, join B in 2nd sc of corner, ch 4 (counts as dc plus ch 1), *sk 1 st, 2-dc cl in next st, ch 1; rep from * across, ending with dc in last st, turn. (53 2-dc cl, 2 dc, 54 ch-1 sps)

Row 2: Ch 3, (2-dc cl, ch 1) in each ch-1 sp, ending with 2-dc cl in last ch-1 sp, dc in last st, turn. (54 2-dc cl, 2 dc, 53 ch-1 sp)

Change to E.

Row 3: Ch 1, sc in each st and ch-1 sp across, turn. (109 sc)

Row 4: Ch 1, sc in first st, *ch 3, sk 3 sts, sc in next st; rep from * across, turn.

Change to C.

Row 5: Ch 3, (2 dc, hdc, sc) in next ch-3 sp, (sc, ch 3, 2 dc, hdc, sc) in each ch-3 sp across, sc in last sc, turn.

Change to E.

Row 6: Ch 6, sk first 5 sts, (sc, ch 3) in each ch-3 sp across to last ch-3 sp, sc in 3rd ch of turning ch, turn.

Change to D.

Row 7: Ch 1, sc in first st, ch 4, bobble in last sc made, sc in next sc, ch 4, bobble in sc, *sc in next sc, ch 4, bobble in last sc made, sk next 2 sc; rep from * across to turning ch, sc in 3rd ch of turning ch, turn.

Change to A.

Row 8: Ch 3, (3 dc, ch 1) in each ch-4 sp across, ending with dc in last st, turn.

Row 9: Ch 4, dc3tog, *ch 3, dc3tog over next 3 dc; rep from * across to last 3 dc, ch 1, dc in last st, turn.

Change to C.

Row 10: Ch 3, dc in first dc, ch 1, sk next ch-1 sp, (3 dc, ch 1) in each ch-3 sp across, 2 dc in 3rd ch of turning ch, turn.

Row 11: Ch 3, dc in next dc, ch 3, *dc3tog over next 3 dc, ch 3; rep from * across to last 2 sts, dc2tog over last 2 sts, turn.

Change to E.

Row 12: Ch 3, dc in ch-3 sp, dc in next st *(ch 1, dc, ch 1) in ch-3 sp, dc in next st; rep from * across, turn.

Row 13: Ch 3, dc in each ch-1 sp across, turn.

Row 14: Ch 4, *sk 1, ch 1, dc in next st; rep from * across, turn.

Change to B.

Row 15: Ch 2, hdc in each st and ch-1 sp across, turn.

Change to A.

Row 16: Ch 2, hdc in back horizontal bar of each hdc across.

Repeat Rows 1–14 in the following order:

Row 17: Rep Row 1 in D.

Row 18: Rep Row 2 in D.

Row 19: Rep Row 3 in C.

Row 20: Rep Row 4 in C.

Row 21: Rep Row 5 in A.

Row 22: Rep Row 6 in C.

Row 23: Rep Row 7 in B.

Row 24: Rep Row 8 in E.

Row 25: Rep Row 9 in E.

Row 26: Rep Row 10 in A.

Row 27: Rep Row 11 in A.

Row 28: Rep Row 12 in C.

Row 29: Rep Row 13 in C.

Row 30: Rep Row 14 in C.

Row 31: Rep Row 1 in B.

Row 32: Rep Row 2 in B. Fasten off.

Sew panel 2 onto the end of Row 32.

Border

Rnd 1: With RS facing, join C in first st in corner on right side, (ch 2, dc) in same st (counts as first cl), ch 3, 2-dc cl in same sp, *ch 1, sk 1 st, cl in next st; rep from * across to last st of row, (cl, ch 3, cl) in last st, working evenly across edge [(cl, ch 1) sk 1 st] across to opposite edge; (cl , ch 3, cl) in first st of end of row, [ch 1, sk 1 st, cl in next st] across edge to last st, (cl, ch 3, cl) in last st, working evenly across edge [(cl, ch 1) sk 1 st] across to opposite edge; join with sl st to first cl. Fasten off.

Rnd 2: With E, join in ch-3 sp, ch 1, 3 sc in same sp, sc in each st and ch-1 sp with 3 sc in each ch-3 sp; join with sl st to first sc.

Fasten off.

Blueberry Bliss

A solid yarn worked in a clever pattern creates an eye-catching effect. This is great for beginners who want a fast and easy blanket . . . but with pattern interest!

Yarn
Caron Simply Soft; medium weight #4; 100% acrylic; 6 oz (170 g)/315 yds (288 m) per skein
2 skeins: Cobalt Blue

Hooks and Other Materials
US size M-13 (9 mm) crochet hook
Yarn needle

Finished Measurements
29 in. (73.5 cm) wide and 46 in. (117 cm) long

Gauge
11 dc and 5 rows = 4 in. (10 cm)

Special Stitches
Cluster (cl): *Yo, insert hook in st, yo, pull up lp; rep from * twice more, yo, pull through all lps on hook.

Pattern Notes
• The beginning ch 3 counts as the first dc.

INSTRUCTIONS
Ch 127.

Row 1 (RS): Dc in 4th ch from hook, dc in next 3 ch, *ch 1, sk next ch, dc in next 3 ch; rep from * to end of row, dc in last st, turn. (80 dc, 13 ch-1 sps)

Row 2: Ch 3, *sk 1 dc, (cl, ch 3, cl) in next st; rep from * in center st of each dc group across, ending with dc in last st, turn.
Row 3: Ch 3, (work 3 dc, ch 1) in each ch-3 sp across row, ending with dc in last st, turn.
Rows 4–32: Rep Rows 2 and 3, ending on Row 2.

Border
Rnd 1: [Ch 3, turn, sl st in next ch-3 sp] across to last ch-3 sp, turn to work along side edge, [ch 3, sl st in end of next row] across to Row 1, [ch 3, sl st in next ch-1 sp] across; turn to work along side edge [ch 3, sl st to end of next row] across; join with sl st to first ch.
Rnd 2: Sl st to next ch-3 sp, *ch 4, sl st to next ch-3 sp; rep from * around; join with sl st to first ch-3 sp. Fasten off.

Finishing
Weave in ends.

Rosebud Blanket

Roses are red. Violets are blue. This pattern is quick and easy to do!

Yarn
Bernat Maker Home Dec; medium weight #4; 100% acrylic; 8.8 oz (250 g)/317 yds (290 m) per skein
1 skein each: 110009 Cream (**A**), 11003 Sweet Pea (**B**), 11001 Woodberry (**C**)

Hooks and Other Materials
US size M-13 (9 mm) crochet hook
Yarn needle

Finished Measurements
24 in. (61 cm) wide and 36 in. (91.5 cm) long

Gauge
12 sts x 4 rows = 4 in. (10 cm)

Special Stitches
V-Stitch (V-st): (Dc, ch 1, dc) in same st or sp.

Pattern Notes
- The beginning ch 2 will not count as a stitch.
- To change yarn color, work last st of old color to last yarn over. Yarn over with new color and draw through all loops on hook to complete st. Fasten off old color. Proceed with new color. (See photo tutorial in Stitch Guide on page 133.)

INSTRUCTIONS
With A, ch 44.
Row 1: Sc in 2nd ch from hook, *sc in next ch, dc in next chain; rep from * across, turn. (43 sts)
Row 2: Ch 1, sc, in each st across, turn.
Change to B.
Row 3: Ch 2, dc in the same st as beg ch 2, sk 2 sts, *V-St in next st, sk 2 sts; rep from * across to last st, dc in last st, turn.
Change to C.

Row 4: Ch 2, 3 dc in the same st as beg ch 2, 3 dc in each ch-1 sp across, ending with dc in last st, turn.

Change to A.

Row 5: Ch 2, dc in the same st as beg ch 2, 2 dc in first sp, *3 dc *over* B and C rows (see photos as reference); rep from * across to last st, dc in last st, turn.

Row 6: Ch 1, sc in each st across, turn.

Rows 7–22: Rep Rows 3–6.

Row 23: Continuing with A, ch 2, dc in the same st as beg ch 2, dc in each st across, turn.

Row 24: Ch 1, sc in each st across, turn.

Rows 25–36: Rep Rows 23 and 24.

Rows 37–48: Rep Rows 3–6.

Rows 49–56: Rep Rows 23 and 24.

Rows 57–60: Rep Rows 3–6. Fasten off.

Border

Rnd 1: Join B in top right corner, ch 3, ch 1, sk 1 st, * dc, ch 1, sk 1 st, rep to last st, (dc, ch 1, dc) in last st, turn to work down side edge in ends of rows [dc, ch 1, sk 1 st] across**, (dc, ch 1, dc) in first st of Row 1; rep from * around, ending at **; join with sl st to beg ch 3.

Rnd 2: Join C in first ch-1 space, *ch 3, sl st in next ch-1 space, rep to corner, (sc, ch 1, sc) in corner; rep from * to complete round; join with sl st to the first space.

Rnd 3: Join C with sl st in first ch-1 sp, [ch 1, (dc, ch 1) twice, sl st] in same sp, *[sl st, ch 1, (dc, ch 1) twice, sl st] in each ch-3 space, V-st in last st, turn to work down side edge, (sc, ch 1) in each ch-3 sp across next row, V-st in first st; rep from * around; join with sl st to the first sl st.

Fasten off.

Finishing

Weave in ends.

Triangle Angel Blanket

If you can make triangles, you can make this blanket! Mix and match your colors to create the coolest geometric blanket!

Yarn

Lion Brand Yarn Vanna's Choice; medium weight #4; 100% acrylic; 3.5 oz (100 g)/170 yds (156 m) per skein

1 skein each: 860-145 Eggplant (**A**), 860-106 Aquamarine (**B**), 860-175 Radiant Lime (**C**), 860-117 Electric Blue (**D**), 860-104 Pink Grapefruit (**E**)

2 skeins: 860-158 Mustard (**F**)

Hooks and Other Materials

US size J-10 (6 mm) crochet hook
Yarn needle

Finished Measurements

32 in. (81 cm) wide and 42 in. (106.5 cm) long

Gauge

12 dc x 6 rows = 4 in. (10 cm)

Special Stitches

Shell: 5 dc in same st or sp.

Pattern Notes

• The beginning ch 3 counts as the first dc.

INSTRUCTIONS

Triangle

Make 18 in A, 20 in B, 14 in C, 12 in D, 14 in E, 18 in F.

Ch 4.

Row 1 (RS): (Dc 2, ch 2, dc 3) in first chain, turn.

Row 2: Ch 3, dc in same st, dc in next 2 sts, (dc, ch 2, dc) in next ch-2 sp, dc in next 2 sts, 2 dc in last st, turn.

Row 3: Ch 3, dc in next 4 sts, (dc, ch 2, dc) in next ch-2 sp, dc in next 4 sts, 2 dc in last st, turn.

Row 4: Ch 3, dc in next 6 sts, (dc, ch 2, dc) in next ch-2 sp, dc in next 6 sts, 2 dc in last st. Fasten off.

Assembly
Use yarn needle to sew triangles together, using illustration as a guide.

Border
Rnd 1: With RS facing, join F in corner ch-2 sp, (ch 3, dc, ch 1, 2 dc) in ch-2 sp, *sk 1 st, [(2 dc, ch 1, 2 dc) in next st, sk 2 sts] rep across to next corner ch-2 sp**, (2 dc, ch 1, 2 dc) in next st; turn to work down edge using ends of rows as sts; rep from * around, ending last rep at **; join with sl st to beg ch 3.

Rnd 2: Ch 3, 4 dc in ch-1 space, sl st between the 2 dc sets, *shell in next ch-1 space, sl st between the 2 dc sets; rep from * around; join with a sl st to beg ch 3.

Fasten off.

Finishing
Weave in ends.

Cutiekins Blanket

A great blanket for learning new stitches, this striped crochet sampler has a fun striped side border.

Yarn

Cascade 220 Superwash Aran; medium weight #4; 100% superwash merino wool; 3.5 oz (100 g)/150 yds (137.5 m) per skein

6 skeins: 274 Chili (**A**)

2 skeins each: 272 White Sand (**B**), 837 Extra Cream Cafe (**C**)

Hooks and Other Materials

US size I-9 (5.5 mm) crochet hook

Yarn needle

Finished Measurements

36 in. (91.5 cm) wide and 48 in. (122 cm) long

Gauge

14 sts x 16 rows = 4 in. (10 cm) in sc

Special Stitches

Cluster (cl): *Yo, insert hook in st, yo, pull up lp; rep from * twice more, yo, pull through all lps on hook.

2-dc cluster: *Yo, insert hook in st, yo, pull up lp; rep from * once more, yo, pull through all lps on hook.

3-dc puff st: (Yo, insert hook in next st, yo, draw through st, yo, draw yarn through 2 lps on hook) 3 times in same st, yo, draw through 4 lps on hook.

Pattern Notes

- The beginning ch 3 counts as the first dc unless otherwise noted.
- To change yarn color, work last st of old color to last yarn over. Yarn over with new color and draw through all loops on hook to complete st. Fasten off old color. Proceed with new color. (See photo tutorial in Stitch Guide on page 133.)

INSTRUCTIONS

Middle Section

With A, ch 69.

Row 1 (RS): Dc in 4th ch from hook and in each ch across, turn. (67 dc)

Row 2: Ch 1, sc in first dc and in each across, ending with last sc in 3rd ch of turning ch, turn.

Row 3: Ch 1, (sc, ch 3, 3-dc puff st) in first sc, *skip next 2 sc**, (sc, ch 3, 3-dc puff st) in next sc; rep from * across, ending last rep at **, sc in last sc, turn.

Row 4: Ch 3 (counts as hdc and ch 1), skip next puff st, sc in next ch-3 sp, (ch 3, sc) in each ch-3 sp across to last ch-3 sp, hdc in last sc, turn.

Row 5: Ch 3, skip first hdc, *dc in next sc, 2 dc in next ch-3 sp; rep from * across to turning ch, dc in ch-1 sp of turning ch, dc in 3rd ch of turning ch, turn.

Rows 6–108: Rep Rows 2–5, ending on Row 4.

Sides

Use ends of rows as sts.

Row 1 (RS): With B, ch 3, *2-dc cl, ch 1, sk 1; rep from * across, ending with dc in last st, turn.

Row 2: Ch 3, *cl in next ch-1 sp, ch 1; rep from * across, ending with last st, turn.

Change to A.

Row 3: Ch 1, sc in each st and ch-1 sp across, turn.

Change to C.

Rows 5 and 6: Rep Rows 1 and 2.

Change to A.

Row 7: Rep Row 3.

Change to B.

Rows 8 and 9: Rep Rows 1 and 2.

Change to A.

Row 10: Rep Row 3.

Fasten off.

Finishing

Add 3 in. (7.5 cm) tassels made in C on each corner. Cut a 12 in. (30.5 cm) length of C for ties. Thread into blunt needle. Wrap a double strand of C around 3 in. (7.5 cm) cardboard 20 times. Insert needle under all strands at upper edge of cardboard. Pull tightly and knot securely near strands. Use these ends to attach tassel to blanket. Cut yarn loops at lower edge of cardboard. Wrap strand of C tightly around loops 1 in. (2.5 cm) below top knot. Knot securely; thread ends into needle and weave into center of tassel. Trim tassel ends evenly.

Weave in ends.

Speckled Blanket

Wow! Mix a stitch sampler with an exciting yarn and watch that blanket turn into something stunning!

Yarn

Cascade 220 Superwash Aran Splatter; medium weight #4; 100% superwash merino wool; 3.5 oz (100 g)/150 yds (137.5 m) per skein

5 skeins: 16 Spring Bouquet

Hooks and Other Materials

US size I-9 (5.5 mm) crochet hook

Yarn needle

Finished Measurements

28 in. (71 cm) wide and 34 in. (86.5 cm) long

Gauge

14 sts x 16 rows = 4 in. (10 cm) in sc

Pattern Notes

- The beginning ch 3 counts as the first dc.
- The beginning ch 4 counts as the first dc plus ch 1, unless otherwise noted.

INSTRUCTIONS

Ch 91.

Row 1 (RS): Dc in 4th ch from hook and in each ch across, turn. (89 sts)

Row 2: Ch 4, sk next dc, *dc in next dc, ch 1, sk next dc; rep from * across to turning ch, dc in 3rd ch of turning ch, turn. (45 dc, 44 ch-1 sps)

Row 3: Ch 3, *dc in next ch-1 sp, dc in next dc; rep from * across, ending with last dc in 3rd ch of turning ch, turn. (89 sts)

Row 4: Ch 1, sc in first dc, ch 1, sk next dc, *sc in next dc, ch 1, sk next dc; rep from * across to turning ch, sc in 3rd ch of turning ch, turn. (45 sc, 44 ch-1 sps)

Row 5: Ch 3, *dc in next ch-1 sp, dc in next sc; rep from * across, turn. (89 sts)

Row 6: Ch 3, sk next dc, dc in next dc, ch 3, 3 dc around the post of last dc made to create a wrapped st, *sk next 3 dc, dc in next dc, ch 3, 3 dc around the post of last dc made; rep from * 21 times, sk next dc, dc in 3rd ch of turning ch, turn. (22 wrapped dc groups, 2 dc)

Row 7: Ch 4 (counts as tr), *sk next 3 dc, dc in top of next ch-3 sp, ch 3, 3 dc around the post of last dc made; rep from * across to turning ch, tr in turning ch, turn. (22 cl, 2 tr)

Row 8: Ch 4, *sk next 3 dc, sc in top of next ch-3 sp**, ch 3; rep from * across, ending last rep at **, ch 1, dc in 4th ch of turning ch, turn. (22 sc, 21 ch-3 sps, 2 ch-1 sps, 2 dc)

Row 9: Ch 3, dc in next ch-1 sp, *dc in next sc, 3 dc in ch-3 sp; rep from * across to last ch-3 sp, dc in next sc, dc in ch-1 sp of turning ch, dc in 3rd ch of turning ch, turn. (89 sts)

Rows 10 and 11: Ch 3, *sk next dc, dc in next dc, dc in skipped dc; rep from * across to last st, dc in 3rd ch of turning ch, turn.

Row 12: Rep Row 2.

Row 13: Ch 1, sc in first dc, sk first ch-1, (sc, ch 3, sc) in each ch-1 sp across, ending with sc in last dc, turn.

Row 14: Ch 4, (dc, ch 1) in each ch-3 sp, ending with dc in last sc, turn.

Row 15: Rep Row 13.

Row 16: Rep Row 14.

Rows 17–51: Rep Rows 3–16 two more times then repeat rows 3–9.

Rows 52: Rep Row 3.

Row 53: Ch 3, dc in each st across. Fasten off.

Border

Rnd 1: Ch 1, 3 sc in first st, sc evenly along side edge to next corner, work 3 sc in last sc, turn to work along side edge, sc evenly across, work 3 sc in first st of Row 1, sc evenly across to last st, 3 sc in last st, turn to work along side edge, sc evenly across, join with a sl st to first sc; ending with even number of sts.

Rnd 2: Sl st to second sc of corner, ch 4, dc in same st, ch 1, sk 1 st, [dc in next st, ch 1, sk 1 st] across to last st, (dc, ch 1, dc) in corner, ch 1, sk 1 st, [dc in next st, ch 1, sk 1 st] across, (dc, ch 1, dc) in 2nd sc of corner, ch 1, sk 1 st, [dc in next st, ch 1, sk 1 st] across to last st, (dc, ch 1, dc) in 2nd sc of corner, ch 1, sk 1 st, [dc in next st, ch 1, sk 1 st] across to last st; join with sl st to 3rd ch of beg ch 4.

Rnd 3: Ch 1, sc in each st and ch-1 sp with 3 sc in each ch-1 sp in corners; join with a sl st to first sc. Fasten off.

Finishing

Weave in ends.

Cuddle and Play

Mixing two simple components together can make a great impact. Mix and match your colors and stitches to create this fantastic blanket.

Yarn

Red Heart Soft Baby Steps; medium weight #4; 100% acrylic; 5 oz (141 g)/256 yds (234 m) per skein

3 skeins each: E746-9600 White (**A**), E746-9505 Aqua (**B**), E746-9939 Tickle (**C**)

Hooks and Other Materials

US size J-10 (6 mm) crochet hook
Yarn needle

Finished Measurements

30 in. (76 cm) wide and 50 in. (127 cm) long

Gauge

14 sts x 16 rows = 4 in. (10 cm) in sc

Pattern Notes

- The blanket is made in two-section panels. After each panel is made, they will be sewn together to create the body of the blanket. A border will be added to finish.
- The beginning ch 5 counts as the first dc plus ch 2.

INSTRUCTIONS

Panel

Horizontal Section: Make 3 in A, 2 in B.

Ch 69.

Row 1 (RS): Sc in 7th ch from hook, ch 2, sk next ch, dc in next ch, *ch 2, sk next ch, sc in next ch, ch 2, sk next ch, dc in next ch; rep from * across, turn. (33 sts, 33 ch-sps)

Row 2: Ch 2, sc in first dc, *sk next ch-2 sp, (dc, ch 3, dc) in next sc, sk next ch-2 sp, sc in next dc; rep from * across, ending with last sc in 3rd ch of turning ch, turn.

Row 3: Ch 5, sc in next ch-3 sp, ch 2, dc in next sc, *ch 2, sc in next ch-3 sp, dc in next sc; rep from * across, turn.

Rows 4–23: Rep Rows 2 and 3.

Fasten off.

Vertical Side Section

<u>For A panels:</u>

Row 1 (RS): With RS facing, turn to work down left edge, join C on edge, ch 1, sc in each st across, turn. (about 25 sts)

Row 2: Ch 1, sc in first st, *dc in next st, sc in next st; rep from * across, turn.

Row 3: Ch 1, sc in each st across, turn.

Rows 4–39: Rep Rows 2 and 3.

Fasten off.

<u>For B panels:</u>

Row 1 (RS): With RS facing, turn to work down right edge, join C on edge, ch 1, sc in each st across, turn. (about 25 sts)

Row 2: Ch 1, sc in first st, *dc in next st, sc in next st; rep from * across, turn.

Row 3: Ch 1, sc in each st across, turn.

Rows 4–39: Rep Rows 2 and 3.

Fasten off.

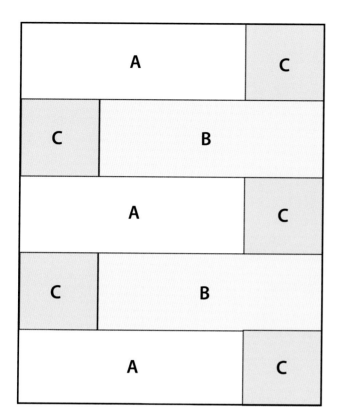

After all panels have been created, sew panels together using illustration as a guide.

Border

Rnd 1: With RS facing, join A in last st on top left corner, ch 3, turn to work along side edge, dc evenly along that edge to next corner, work 3 dc in first sc of Row 1, dc evenly across to last st, work 3 dc in last st, dc evenly along remaining edge, work dc in first sc of top row, sc evenly across top edge to last st, work 2 dc in last st; join with a sl st to beg ch 3.

Rnd 2: Ch 3, dc in each st with 3 dc in each corner; join with a sl st to beg ch 3.

Change to B.

Rnd 3: Ch 3, dc in each st with 3 dc in each corner; join with a sl st to beg ch 3.

Fasten off.

Finishing

Weave in ends.

Sherbet Squares

Learn new stitches and work them in blocks. Use your favorite yarn and have fun making this stunning stitch sampler.

Yarn
Cascade Anthem; medium weight #4; 100% acrylic; 3.5 oz (100 g)/186 yds (170 m) per skein
3 skeins each: 23 Tangerine (**A**), 33 Cocatro (**B**), 19 Lime (**C**)

Hooks and Other Materials
US size J-10 (6 mm) crochet hook
Yarn needle

Finished Measurements
33 in. (84 cm) wide and 58 in. (147 cm) long

Gauge
14 sts x 16 rows = 4 in. (10 cm) in sc

Special Stitches
Treble Cluster (tr cl): *Yo 2 times, insert hook in stitch and draw up a lp; (yo and draw through 2 lps on hook) twice; rep from * once, yo and draw through 3 lps.

Cluster (cl): Yo, insert hook in st and draw up a lp, yo and draw through 2 lps on hook; yo and insert hook in same st and draw up a lp, yo and draw through 2 lps on hook; yo and draw through 3 lps on hook.

Shell: 5 dc in specified st or space.

Popcorn stitch (PC): Work 5 dc in specified st; drop lp from hook, insert hook from front to back in top of first dc of 5-dc group; insert hook in dropped lp and draw lp through, ch 1.

Reverse Single Crochet (rev sc): Sc worked from left to right (right to left, if left-handed). Insert hook into next stitch to the right (left), under lp on hook, and draw up a lp. Yo, draw through all lps on hook. (See photo tutorial in Stitch Guide on page 150.)

Pattern Notes
- The beginning ch 3 counts as the first dc.
- The beginning ch 4 counts as the first dc plus ch 1, unless otherwise noted.

INSTRUCTIONS

Block 1
Make 4.

With A, ch 32.

Row 1 (RS): Sc in 2nd ch from hook and in each ch across, turn. (31 sc)

Row 2: Ch 4 (counts as tr), *sk 2 sc, (tr cl, ch 1, tr cl) in next sc; rep from * across to last 2 sts, sk 1 st, tr in last st, turn.

Rows 3–10: Ch 4 (counts as tr), (tr cl, ch 1, tr cl) in ch-1 sp of each group across to last st, tr in top of turning ch, turn.

Row 11: Ch 1, sc in each st across, do not turn.

Trim:

Rnd 1: Ch 1, working along side edge, sc 30 evenly along the edge to next corner, work 3 sc in first sc of Row 1, sc evenly across to last st, work 3 sc in last st, sc 30 evenly along remaining edge, work 3 sc in first sc of Row 27, sc evenly across top edge to last st, work 3 sc in last st, sl st to first sc to join.

Fasten off.

Block 2
Make 4.

With B, Ch 32.

Row 1 (RS): Sc in 2nd ch from hook and in each ch across, turn. (31 sc)

Row 2: Ch 3, *sk next sc, cl in next sc; working in front of cl just made, cl in skipped sc, dc in next sc; rep from * across, turn.

Row 3: Ch 1, sc in each st across, turn.

Rows: 4–27: Rep Rows 2 and 3.

Trim:

Rnd 1: Ch 1, working along side edge, sc 30 evenly to next corner, work 3 sc in first sc of Row 1, sc evenly across to last st, work 3 sc in last st, sc 30 evenly along remaining side edge, work 3 sc in first sc of Row 27, sc evenly across top edge to last st, work 3 sc in last st, sl st to first sc to join.

Fasten off.

Block 3

Make 4.

With C, ch 32.

Row 1 (RS): Sc in 2nd ch from hook and in each ch across, turn. (31 sc)

Row 2: Ch 1, sc in first sc, *sk 2 sc, shell in next sc, sk 2 sc, PC in next sc; rep from * to last 6 sts, sk 2 sc, shell in next sc, sk 2 sc, dc in last sc, turn.

Row 3: Ch 3, *sc in center dc of next shell, ch 2, sc in next PC, ch 2; rep from * across, ending with sc in center dc of last shell, ch 2, dc in last sc.

Row 4: Ch 3, *shell in next sc, PC in next sc; rep from * across, ending with a shell in last sc, dc in turning ch, turn.

Row 5: Rep Row 3, ending with sc in top of turning ch.

Rows 6–21: Rep Rows 4 and 5.

Trim:

Rnd 1: Ch 1, sc 30 evenly along side edge to next corner, work 3 sc in first sc of Row 1, sc evenly across to last st, work 3 sc in last st, sc 30 evenly along remaining side edge, work 3 sc in first sc of Row 21, sc evenly across top edge to last st, work 3 sc in last st, sl st to first sc to join.

Fasten off.

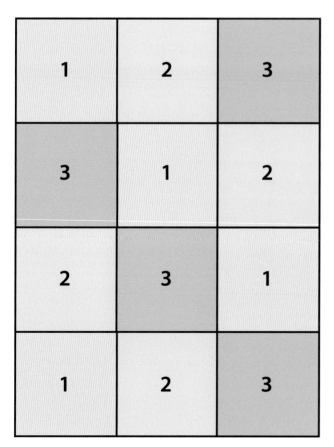

Assembly

Sew all squares together using illustration as a guide.

Border

Rnd 1: With RS facing, join A in last st on top left, ch 3, turn to work along side edge, dc evenly along edge to next corner, work 3 dc in first sc of Row 1, dc evenly across to last st, work 3 dc in last st, dc 30 evenly along remaining side edge, work 3 dc in first dc of top row, dc evenly across top edge to last st, work 2 dc in last st; join with sl st to beg ch 3.

Row 2: Ch 3, 2 dc in same st, dc in each st around, working 3 dc in 2nd dc in each corner; join with sl st to first dc.

Change to B.

Row 3: Ch 1, reverse sc in each st around; join with sl st to first sc.

Fasten off.

Finishing

Weave in ends.

Honeydew Blanket

This blanket is all about practicing the basics. With only two colors and a few stitches, this sampler is a great place to start mastering your techniques.

Yarn
Knit Picks Comfy Worsted; medium weight #4; 75% pima cotton/25% acrylic; 5 oz (50 g)/109 yds (100 m) per skein
3 skeins each: 24152 Honeydew (**A**), 24162 Ivory (**B**)

Hooks and Other Materials
US size J-10 (6 mm) crochet hook
Yarn needle

Finished Measurements
28 in. (71 cm) wide and 48 in. (122 cm) long

Gauge
8 sts x 3 rows = 2 in. (5 cm) in dc

Special Stitches
Cluster (cl): *Yo, insert hook in st or sp indicated, yo and pull up a lp, yo and draw through 2 lps on hook; rep from * 2 times more, yo and draw through all 4 lps on hook.

INSTRUCTIONS

With A, ch 91.

Row 1 (RS): (Cl, ch 1, cl) in 7th ch from hook, *sk next 2 chs, (4 dc, ch 1, dc) in next ch, sk 5 chs, (cl, ch 1, cl) in next ch; rep from * across to last 3 chs, ch 1, sk next 2 chs, dc in last ch; turn.

Row 2: Ch 4, sk first ch-1 sp, (cl, ch 1, cl) in next ch-1 sp, *(4 dc, ch 1, dc) in next ch-1 sp, (cl, ch 1, cl) in next ch-1 sp; rep from * across to last 2 chs, ch 1, sk next ch, dc in last ch; turn.

Rows 3 and 4: Rep Row 2. Fasten off A, join B.

Rows 5 and 6: Rep Row 2. Fasten off B, join A.

Rows 7–10: Rep Row 2. Fasten off A, join B

Rows 11–70: Rep Rows 5–10. Do not turn at end of Row 70.

Border

Rnd 1: Ch 1, sc evenly across ends of rows, 3 sc in the first st of Row 1, sc to last st, 3 sc in last st of Row 1, sc evenly across ends of rows to Row 70, 3 sc in the first st of Row 70, sc to last st, 3 sc in last st, join with a sl st to first sc.

Finishing

Weave in ends.

Asher Log Cabin

Crocheted from the center outward, this blocky blanket is a showstopper! Not only are the stitches interesting to crochet but it's exciting to watch the blanket grow.

Yarn
Lion Brand Yarn Touch of Alpaca; medium weight #4; 90% acrylic/10% alpaca; 7 oz (200 g)/415 yds (380 m) per skein
1 skein each: 674-146 Purple Aster (**A**), 674-123 Taupe (**B**), 674-098 Cream (**C**)

Hooks and Other Materials
US size J-10 (6 mm) crochet hook
Yarn needle

Finished Measurements
34 in. (86.5 cm) wide and 34 in. (86.5 cm) long

Gauge
14 sts x 16 rows = 4 in. (10 cm) in sc

Pattern Notes
- The beginning ch 3 counts as the first dc.
- The beginning ch 4 counts as the first dc plus ch 1.
- To change yarn color, work last st of old color to last yarn over. Yarn over with new color and draw through all loops on hook to complete st. Fasten off old color. Proceed with new color. (See photo tutorial in Stitch Guide on page 133.)

INSTRUCTIONS

Section 1
With A, ch 18.

Row 1 (RS): Sc in 2nd ch from hook and in each across, turn. (17 sc)

Row 2: Ch 1, sc in first sc, *ch 3, sk 3 sts, sc in next sc; rep from * across, turn.

Row 3: Ch 4, *3 tr in ch-sp, yo twice, insert hook in space at right of 3rd tr from hook, pull up a lp and finish as a tr, tr in next sc; rep from * across, turn.

Row 4: Ch 1, sc in first tr, *ch 3, sk next 4 tr, sc in next tr; rep from * across, turn.

Rows 5–10: Rep Rows 3 and 4.

Row 11: Ch 1, sc in first tr, *3 sc in ch-3 sp, sc in next tr; rep from * across.

Change to B.

Section 2
Row 1: Ch 1, turn to work along side edge, sc 17 across, turn.

Rows 2–11: Rep Rows 2–11 from Section 1.

Section 3
Row 1: Turn to work along side edge, sc 17 across, turn.

Rows 2–11: Rep Rows 2–11 from Section 1.

Section 4
Row 1: Turn to work along side edge, sc 33 across, turn.

Rows 2–11: Rep Rows 2–11 from Section 1.

Section 5
Row 1: Turn to work along side edge, sc 49 across, turn.

Rows 2–11: Rep Rows 2–11 from Section 1.

Change to C.

Section 6
Row 1: Turn to work along side edge, sc 49 across, turn.

Rows 2–11: Rep Rows 2–11 from Section 1.

Section 7
Row 1: Turn to work along side edge, sc 65 across, turn.

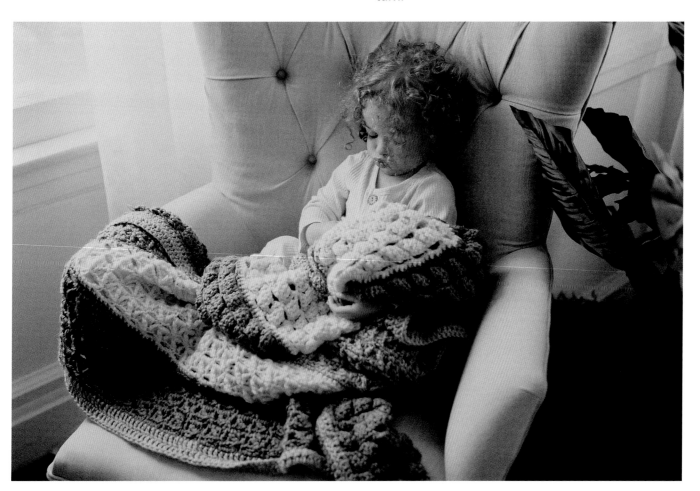

Rows 2–11: Rep Rows 2–11 from Section 1.

Section 8
Row 1: Turn to work along side edge, sc 65 across, turn.
Rows 2–11: Rep Rows 2–11 from Section 1.

Section 9
Row 1: Turn to work along side edge, sc 81 across, turn.
Rows 2–11: Rep Rows 2–11 from Section 1.
Change to A.

Section 10
Row 1: Turn to work along side edge, sc 81 across, turn.
Rows 2–11: Rep Rows 2–11 from Section 1.

Section 11
Row 1: Turn to work along side edge, sc 97 across, turn.
Rows 2–11: Rep Rows 2–11 from Section 1.

Section 12
Row 1: Turn to work along side edge, sc 97 across, turn.
Rows 2–11: Rep Rows 2–11 from Section 1.

Section 13
Row 1: Turn to work along side edge, sc 113 across, turn.
Rows 2–11: Rep Rows 2–11 from Section 1.
Change to B.

Border
Rnd 1: Ch 3, *turn to work along side edge, dc in each st across, 3 dc in first st of next edge, dc in each st across, 3 dc in last st; rep from * across; join with a sl st to beg ch 3.
Rnd 2: Ch 3, dc in each st around with 3 dc in each corner; join with a sl st to beg ch 3.
Fasten off.

Finishing
Weave in ends.

Rock-a-Bye-Baby Blanket

Made with the softest bulky yarn, this stitch sampler will be sure to keep your hook busy!

Yarn

Premier Anti Pilling Bamboo Chunky; bulky weight #5; 80% acrylic/20% rayon from bamboo; 3.5 oz (100 g)/131 yds (120 m) per skein

3 skeins each: 1085-04 Earl Grey (**A**), 1085-09 Apricot (**B**), 1085-01 Mochi (**C**)

Hooks and Other Materials

US size K-10½ (6.5 mm) crochet hook
Yarn needle

Finished Measurements

35 in. (89 cm) wide and 47 in. (119.5 cm) long

Gauge

14 sts x 16 rows = 4 in. (10 cm) in sc

Special Stitches

Cluster (cl): (Yo) 3 times, insert hook in indicated ch and draw up a lp, (yo and draw through 2 lps on hook) 3 times, *(yo) 3 times, insert hook in same ch and draw up a lp, (yo and draw through 2 lps on hook) 3 times; rep from * once more, yo and draw through all lps on hook.

Shell: 5 dc in same st.

Puff stitch (puff st): Worked all in one st: Yo, insert hook in indicated st, yo and draw up a lp, (yo, insert hook in same st, yo and draw up a lp) 4 times, yo, draw through all lps on hook.

Reverse single crochet (rev sc): Single crochet worked from left to right (right to left, if left-handed). Insert hook into next stitch to the right (left), under lp on hook, and draw up a lp. Yo, draw through all lps on hook. (See photo tutorial in Stitch Guide on page 150.)

Pattern Notes

- The beginning ch 2 will not count as a st.
- The beginning ch 3 counts as the first dc.
- The beginning ch 4 counts as the first tr.
- To change yarn color, work last st of old color to last yarn over. Yarn over with new color and draw through all loops on hook to complete st. Fasten off old color. Proceed with new color. (See photo tutorial in Stitch Guide on page 133.)

INSTRUCTIONS

With A, ch 78.

Row 1 (WS): Sc in 2nd ch from hook and in each across, turn. (77 sc)

Row 2 (RS): Ch 1, sc in each st across, turn.

Row 3: Ch 1, sc in first sc, *ch 4, sk next 3 sc, sc in next sc; rep from * across, turn.

Row 4: Ch 4, *2 tr in next ch-4 sp, in sp to right of first tr made (not ch-sp) work 4 dc; rep from * across, ending with tr in last sc, turn.

Row 5: Ch 4, *sk next 4 dc and next tr, sc in next tr, ch 4; rep from * across, ending with sc in top of turning ch, turn.

Row 6: Ch 1, sc in each sc and 3 sc in each ch-4 sp, turn.

Row 7: Ch 1, sc in each st across, turn.

Change to B.

Row 8: Ch 2, 3 dc in first st, *sk next 3 sc, (sc, ch 3, dc) in next sc; rep from * to last 4 sts, sk 3 sts, sc in last sc, turn.

Row 9: Ch 2, 3 dc in first sc, *sk next dc and ch-3 sp, (sc, ch 3, dc) in next sc; rep from * across to last st, sc in 2nd ch of turning ch, turn.

Rows 10–13: Rep Rows 8 and 9.

Change to C.

Row 14: Ch 1, 2 sc in first st, 3 sc in next ch-3 sp, *sc in each sc, 3 sc in next ch-3 sp; rep from * across to last ch-3 sp, sc in next 2 dc, sk 1 dc, sc in turning ch, turn.

Row 15: Ch 1, turn; sc in first sc, *cl in next sc, sc in next sc; rep from * across, turn.

Row 16: Ch 1, turn; sc in each st across, turn.

Change to B.

Row 17: Ch 3, sk 1 sc, *(dc, ch 1, dc) in next sc, sk next sc, dc in next sc**, sk next sc; rep from * across, ending last rep at **, turn.

Change to A.

Row 18: Ch 3, *(dc, ch 1, dc) in next ch-1 sp, sk next dc**, dc in next dc; rep from * across, ending last rep at **, dc in 3rd ch of turning ch, turn.

Change to B.

Row 19: Rep Row 18.

Change to A.

Row 20: Rep Row 18.

Change to B.

Row 21: Rep Row 18.

Join C.

Row 22: Ch 3, dc in each st and ch across, turn.

Row 23: Ch 3, *sk next dc, dc in next dc, working behind last dc made, dc in last skipped dc (crossed dc made); rep from * across, turn.

Row 24: Ch 3, dc in each st across, turn.

Change to B.

Row 25: Ch 3, sk 1 st, 5 dc in next st, *sk 3 sts, shell in next st; rep from * across to last 2 sts, sk 1 st, dc in last st, turn.

Row 26: Ch 4 (counts as dc and ch-1), *sk 2 dc, sc in next dc, ch 1, dc in sp between 2 shells, ch 1; rep from * across to last shell, sk 2 dc, sc in next dc, ch 1, dc in last st, turn.

Change to A.

Row 27: Ch 1, sc in first st, sc in ch-1 sp, 2 sc in each ch-1 sp to last sp, sc in last sp, sc in 3rd ch of turning ch, turn.

Rows 28–52: Repeat Rows 2–26.

Row 53: Repeat Row 27.

Rows 54–78: Repeat Rows 2–26.

Row 79: Repeat Row 27.

Rows 80–85: Repeat Rows 2–7.

Fasten off.

Border

Rnd 1: With RS facing, join C in first st on top right, ch 1, 3 sc in first st, sc in each st across to last st, 3 sc in last st, turn to work along side edge, sc evenly across edge to next corner, 3 sc in first st of Row 1, sc in each st across to last st, 3 sc in last st, turn to work along side edge, sc evenly across edge to next corner; join with sl st to first sc.

Rnd 2: Ch 2, *[puff st, ch 1, sk 1] rep across to next corner, 3 dc in 2nd sc in corner; rep from * around; join with sl st to first st.

Rnd 3: Ch 1, sc in each st and ch-1 sp, with 3 sc in 2nd dc in each corner; join with sl st to first st.

Change to B.

Rnd 4: Ch 1, reverse sc in each st around; join with sl st to first st.

Fasten off.

Finishing

Weave in ends.

Blossom Motif
Baby Blanket

These pretty motifs are bordered with a beautiful stitch sampler border. Mix and match colors or use your favorite color for all of the motif centers!

Yarn
Lion Brand Yarn Feels Like Butta; medium weight #4; 100% polyester; 3.5 oz (218 g)/218 yds (119 m) per skein
2 skeins: 215-100 White (**E**)
1 skein each: 215-101 Pink Rose (**A**), 215-156 Mint (**B**), 215-149 Pale Grey (**C**), 215-140 Dusty Pink (**D**)

Hooks and Other Materials
US size H-8 (5 mm) crochet hook
Yarn needle

Finished Measurements
32 in. (81 cm) wide and 32 in. (81 cm) long

Gauge
4 sts x 2 rows = 1 in. (2.5 cm) in dc

Special Stitches
Beginning 2 double crochet cluster (Beg 2dcCL): Ch 2, yo, insert needle in same st, yo and draw up a lp, yo, pull through first 2 lps, yo, pull through all lps on hook (counts as one dc).
2 double crochet cluster (2dcCL): Yo, insert needle in next st, yo and draw up a lp, yo, pull through first 2 lps, yo, pull up a lp in the same st, yo and draw through first 2 lps, yo, pull through all lps on hook (counts as one dc).
3 double crochet cluster (3dcCL): Yo, insert needle in next st, yo and draw up a lp, yo, pull through first 2 lps, [yo, pull up a lp in the same st, yo and draw through first 2 lps] twice, yo, pull through all lps on hook (counts as one dc).

Pattern Notes

- The motifs will be made first and sewn together, and then the border will be crocheted around the square.
- The beginning ch 2 will not count as a st.
- The beginning ch 3 counts as the first dc.
- The beginning ch 6 counts as the first dc plus ch 3.
- To change yarn color, work last st of old color to last yarn over. Yarn over with new color and draw through all loops on hook to complete st. Fasten off old color. Proceed with new color. (See photo tutorial in Stitch Guide on page 133.)

INSTRUCTIONS

Motif

Make 3 each with each color A, C, and D for center.
With center color, ch 5, join with sl st to first ch to form ring.

Rnd 1: Ch 2, 9 dc in ring; join with sl st to first dc. (9 dc)

Rnd 2: Beg 2dcCL, ch 2, *2dcCL in next st, ch 2, rep from * around, join with sl st to Beg 2dcCL. (9 cl, 9 ch-2 sps)

Rnd 3: Ch 2, hdc in same st, (dc, ch 3, dc) in ch-2 sp, *hdc in next st, (dc, ch 3, dc) in ch-2 sp; rep from * around, join with sl st to first hdc. Fasten off.

Rnd 4: Join B in ch-3 sp, ch 1, (sc, 2 dc, ch 1, 2 dc, sc) in each ch-3 sp around; join with sl st to first sc. Fasten off.

Rnd 5: Join main color (E) with sl st in ch-1 sp, ch 1, sc in same sp, *ch 3, sk 2 dc, dc between next 2 sts, ch 3 **, sc in ch-1 sp; rep from * around, ending last rep at **, join with sl st to first sc.

Rnd 6: Ch 3, *3 dc in ch-3 sp, dc in next dc, 3 dc in ch-3 sp **, dc in next sc; rep from * around, ending last rep at **, join with sl st to beg ch 3.

Rnd 7: Ch 6, dc in same st, [dc in next 17 sts, (dc, ch 3, dc) in next st] 3 times, dc in next 17 sts; join with sl st to 3rd ch of beg ch 6.

Rnd 8: Sl st to ch-3 sp, ch 3, 4 dc in same sp, *dc in next 4 sts, hdc in next 2 sts, sc in next 7 sts, hdc in next 2 sts, dc in next 4 sts **, 5 dc in ch-3 sp; rep from * around, ending last rep at **; join with sl st to beg ch 3. Fasten off.

Assembly

Use yarn needle to sew motifs together using illustration as a guide.

A	B	C
C	A	B
B	C	A

Border

Rnd 1: Join A in third dc in corner, ch 6 (first dc and ch 3), dc in same sp, *dc 25 along edge of each motif for a total of 75 per side **, (dc, ch 1, dc) in third dc of corner; rep from * around, ending last rep at **, join with sl st to ch 3 of beg ch 6. Fasten off. (308 sts + 4 ch-3 spaces)

Rnd 2: Join D in ch-3 sp, ch 3, 4 dc in same sp, *ch 1, sk 1 st, 3dcCL in next st, [ch 1, sk 1, 3dcCL in next st] across to last st, ch 1, sk last st **, 5 dc in ch-3 sp; rep from * around, ending last rep at **, join with sl st to beg ch 3. Fasten off.

Rnd 3: Join C in third dc in corner, ch 6 (first dc and ch 3), dc in same sp, *3dcCL in next st, ch 1, sk 1, (3dcCL, ch 1) in each ch-1 sp across, sk 1 st, 3dcCL in next st **, (dc, ch 1, dc) in next st; rep from * around, ending last rep at **; join with sl st to 3rd ch of beg ch 6. Fasten off.

Rnd 4: Join A in ch-3 sp, ch 3, 4 dc in same sp, *3dcCL in next st, ch 1, (3dcCL, ch 1) in each ch-1 sp across **, 5 dc in ch-3 sp; rep from * around, ending last rep at **; join with sl st to beg ch 3. Fasten off.

Rnd 5: Join B in third dc in corner, ch 6 (first dc and ch 3), dc in same st, *sk 2 sts, (sc, 2 dc, ch 1, 2 dc, sc) between dc and cluster, [sk 1 ch-sp, (sc, 2 dc, ch 1, 2 dc) in next ch-sp] across to last ch-sp, sk 1 ch-sp, (sc, 2 dc, ch 1, 2 dc, sc) between last cluster and next dc **, sk 2 sts, (dc, ch 1, dc) in third dc of corner; rep from * around, ending last rep at **; join with sl st to 3rd ch of beg ch 6. Fasten off.

Rnd 6: Join E in ch-3 sp, ch 3, 4 dc in same sp, *dc *over* Rnd 5 into Rnd 4 sp into 4th dc of 5-dc corner, ch 2, sc in next ch-1 sp, [ch 2, dc *over* Rnd 5 into Rnd 4 ch-1 sp, ch 2, sc in next ch-1 sp, ch 2], dc *over* Rnd 5 into Rnd 4 2nd dc of 5-dc corner **, 5 dc in ch-3 sp; rep from * around, ending last rep at **; join with sl st to beg ch 3. Fasten off.

Rnd 7: Join D in 3rd dc in corner, ch 6, dc in same st, *dc in next 3 sts, 2 dc in each ch-2 sp across, dc in next 3 sts **, (dc, ch 1, dc) in next st; rep from * around, ending last rep at **; join with sl st to 3rd ch of beg ch 6. Fasten off.

Rnd 8: Join A in ch-3 sp, ch 3, 4 dc in same sp, *[2 dc between next 2 sts] across to next corner **, 5 dc in ch-1 sp; rep from * around, ending last rep at **; join with sl st to beg ch 3. Fasten off.

Rnd 9: Join C in 3rd dc in corner, ch 6, dc in same st, *[2 dc between next 2 sts] across to next corner**, (dc, ch 1, dc) in 3rd dc of corner; rep from * around, ending last rep at **; join with sl st to 3rd ch of beg ch 6. Fasten off.

Rnd 10: Join B in ch-3 sp, ch 3, 4 dc in same sp, *[sk 3 sts, (2 dc, ch 2, 2 dc) in next st] across to last 2 sts, sk 2 sts **, 5 dc in ch-3 sp; rep from * around, ending last rep at **; join with sl st to beg ch 3. Fasten off.

Finishing

Weave in ends.

Cloudberry

Introduce color into your crocheted blankets with this pattern. The shells are fun to crochet and make a huge impact in your blanket!

Yarn

Knit Picks Dishie; medium weight #4; 100% cotton; 3.5 oz (100 g)/190 yds (174 m) per skein

1 skein in each color: 25789 Silver (**A**), 26668 Blush (**B**), 25788 Kenai (**D**), 25790 Begonia (**E**)

3 skeins: 27041 Mint (**C**)

Hooks and Other Materials

US size H-8 (5 mm) crochet hook

Yarn needle

Finished Measurements

31 in. (78.7 cm) wide and 42 in. (107.7 cm) long

Gauge

4 sts x 2 rows = 1 in. (2.5 cm) in dc

Special Stitches

Shell: 9 dc in specified stitch or space

V-stitch (V-st): (Dc, ch 3, dc) in same specified st or sp.

Pattern Notes

- The beginning ch 2 will not count as first st.
- The beginning ch 3 counts as first double crochet.
- The beginning ch 4 counts as first double crochet plus ch 1.
- For photo tutorial on working into the back loop only (blo), see Stitch Guide on page 136.
- When changing colors, complete the stitch until the last pull through; drop working yarn, pull through next color as last pull through to complete color change and finish stitch. (See photo tutorial in Stitch Guide on page 133.)

INSTRUCTIONS

With Color A, ch 106.

Row 1 (RS): Sc in second ch from hook, [sk next 3 chs, shell in next ch, sk next 3 chs, sc in next ch] across, turn. Change to B.

Row 2: Ch 4, dc in same st as beg ch 4, [ch 2, sk next 4 dc, sc in next dc, ch 2, sk next 4 dc, V-st in next sc] across, turn.

Row 3: Ch 3, 4 dc in same st as beg ch 3, sc in next sc, [shell in ch-sp of next V-st, sc in next sc] across, 5 dc in last sc, turn.

Change to C.

Row 4: Ch 1, sc in first st, ch 2, *V-st in next sc, ch 2, sk next 4 dc, sc in next dc **, ch 2; rep from * across, ending last rep at **, turn.

Row 5: Ch 1, sc in first st, [shell in ch-sp of next V-st, sc in next sc] across, turn.

Change to D.

Rows 6 and 7: Rep Rows 2 and 3.

Change to E.

Rows 8 and 9: Rep Rows 4 and 5.

Change to A.

Rows 10 and 11: Rep Rows 2 and 3.

Change to B.

Rows 12 and 13: Rep Rows 4 and 5.

Change to C.

Rows 14 and 15: Rep Rows 2 and 3.

Change to D.

Rows 16 and 17: Rep Rows 4 and 5.

Change to E.

Rows 18 and 19: Rep Rows 2 and 3.

Change to A.

Rows 20 and 21: Rep Rows 4 and 5.

Change to C.

Row 22: Rep Row 2.

Row 23: Ch 3, sk ch-sp, dc in next dc, *2 dc in ch-2 sp, dc in sc, 2 dc in ch-2 sp, dc in dc **, dc in ch-2 sp, dc in dc, rep from * across, ending last rep at **, sk ch-2 sp, dc in last dc, turn. (105 sts)

Row 24: Ch 2, hdc in each st across, turn.

Row 25: Ch 3, working in the blo, dc in each st across.

Rows 26–65: Rep Rows 24 and 25. Fasten off C.

Row 66: Join A, ch 2, hdc in each st across, turn.

Row 67: Ch 3, working in the blo, dc in each st across.

Change to B.

Rows 68 and 69: Rep Rows 24 and 25.

Change to D.
Rows 70 and 71: Rep Rows 24 and 25.
Change to E.
Rows 72 and 73: Rep Rows 24 and 25.
Change to A.
Rows 74–79: Rep Rows 68–73. Fasten off.

Border
With B, join in first stitch of Row 81.
Rnd 1: Ch 1, 3 sc in first st, sc across to last st, 3 sc in last st, sc evenly across ends of rows to Row 1 (NOTE: make sure stitch count is *odd*), 3 sc in first st of Row 1, sc in each ch and st across, 3 sc in last st, sc evenly across ends of rows (NOTE: make sure stitch count is *odd*); join with sl st to first sc. Fasten off B.
Rnd 2: Join E in 2nd sc of 3-sc corner, ch 1, (sc, ch 3, sc) in same st, ch 3, sk 1 st, *[sc in next st, ch 3, sk 1 st] rep across to corner **, (sc, ch 1, sc) in 2nd sc of 3-sc corner, rep from * around, ending last rep at **; join with sl st to first sc. Fasten off E.

Rnd 3: Join A in ch-3 sp in corner, (ch 4, dc, ch 1, dc, ch 1) in same sp, *(dc, ch 1) in each ch-1 sp across to corner ch-3 sp **, (dc, ch 1, dc, ch 1, dc, ch 1) in ch-3 sp, rep from * around, ending last rep at **; join with sl st to ch-3 of beg ch 4. Fasten off A.
Rnd 4: Join D in any dc in corner, *ch 3, sl st in next dc, rep from * around; join with sl st to first dc. Fasten off.

Finishing
Weave in ends.

Happy Time

This pattern will keep you busy with fun stitches and will ensure lots of happy smiles from your little kiddo!

Yarn
Red Heart Amore; medium weight #4; 100% acrylic; 3.5 oz (100 g)/198 yds (181 m) per skein
4 skeins: 817-6638 Restful

Hooks and Other Materials
US size 7 (5.5 mm) crochet hook
Yarn needle

Finished Measurements
28 in. (71 cm) wide and 48 in. (122 cm) long

Gauge
14 sts x 16 rows = 4 in. (10 cm) in sc

Special Stitches
Double crochet 2 sts together (dc2tog): (Yo, insert hook in next st and draw up a lp, yo and draw through 2 lps) twice, yo and draw through all 3 lps on hook (1 st decreased). (See photo tutorial in Stitch Guide on page 142.)

2 double crochet cluster (2dcCL): Yo, pull up a lp in next st, yo, pull through first 2 lps, yo, pull up a lp in the same st, yo and draw through first 2 lps, yo, pull through all lops on hook (counts as one dc).

Pattern Notes
- The beginning ch 3 counts as the first dc.
- The beginning ch 4 counts as the first dc plus ch 1.

INSTRUCTIONS
Ch 110.

Row 1 (RS): Dc in 6th ch from hook, *ch 1, sk next ch, dc in next ch, rep from * across, turn. (107 sts)

Row 2: Ch 3, dc2tog using same st as beg ch 3 and next dc, *ch 1, dc2tog using same dc and next dc, rep from * across to turning ch, dc in 4th ch of turning ch, turn.

Row 3: Ch 4, (dc, ch 1) in each ch-1 sp across, dc in 3rd ch of turning ch, turn.

Rows 4–9: Rep Rows 2 and 3.

Row 10: Ch 3, dc in each st and ch across, turn.

Row 11: Ch 3, dc in next 2 sts, *ch 1, sk 1 st, dc in next 3 sts; rep from * across, turn.

Row 12: Rep Row 10.

Row 13: Ch 4, sk next dc, dc in next st, *ch 1, sk 1 st, dc in next st; rep from * across, turn.

Rows 14–20: Rep Rows 10–13, ending on Row 12.

Row 18: Rep Row 2.

Row 19: Rep Row 10.

Row 20: Ch 3, *sk next dc, dc in next 2 dc, dc around last 2 dc posts made, rep from * across to last 2 sts, sk 1 st, dc in last st, turn.

Row 21: Rep Row 10.

Rows 22–33: Rep Rows 18–21 three times.

Row 34: Ch 4, sk 1 st, dc in next st, ch 1, *work ½ 2dcCL in next st, sk 1 st and finish cluster in next st, ch 1**, (dc, ch1, sk 1 st) three times, dc in next st; rep from * across ending last rep at **, (dc in next st, ch 1, sk 1) twice, dc in last st, turn.

Row 35: Ch 3, dc in each st and ch across, turn.

Rows 36–44: Rep Rows 34 and 35, ending on Row 34.

Rows 45–48: Ch 3, dc in each st across, turn.

Rows 49–57: Rep Rows 34 and 35, ending on Row 34.

Row 58: Rep Row 10.

Row 59 and 60: Rep Rows 20 and 21.

Rows 61–70: Rep Rows 18–21, ending on Row 19.

Rows 71–73: Rep Rows 11–13.

Rows 74–82: Rep Rows 10–13, ending on Row 10.

Row 83: Rep Row 3.

Rows 84–92: Rep Rows 2 and 3, ending on Row 2.

Fasten off.

Finishing

Weave in ends.

Ethelyn Dreams Blankie

You'll make this blanket in sections: middle and then sides.

Yarn

Berroco Vintage; medium weight #4; 52% acrylic/40% wool/8% nylon; 3.5 oz (100 g)/218 yds (199 m) per skein

6 skeins: 5176 Pumpkin (**A**)

2 skeins each: 5101 Mochi (**B**), 5130 Taupe (**C**)

Hooks and Other Materials

US size J-10 (6 mm) crochet hook

Yarn needle

Finished Measurements

28 in. (71 cm) wide and 50 in. (127 cm) long

Gauge

Rows 1–4 = 4 in. (10 cm)

Special Stitches

Hdc in back horizontal bar: Locate the *top* loops you normally crochet into. On the WS (or back side) of the hdc, you'll see a horizontal bar. Work your hdc into this bar. (See photo tutorial in Stitch Guide on page 138.)

Pattern Notes

- The beginning ch 3 counts as the first dc.
- The beginning ch 4 counts as the first dc plus ch 1.

- To change yarn color, work last st of old color to last yarn over. Yarn over with new color and draw through all loops on hook to complete st. Fasten off old color. Proceed with new color. (See photo tutorial in Stitch Guide on page 133.)

INSTRUCTIONS

Center Section

With C, ch 124.

Row 1 (RS): (4 dc, ch 3, dc) in 6th ch from hook, *sk next 4 chs, (4 dc, ch 3, dc) in next ch; rep from * across to last 3 chs, sk next 2 chs, dc in last ch, turn.

Row 2: Ch 3, (4 dc, ch 3, dc) in each ch-3 sp across to last ch-3 sp, sk next 4 dc, dc in top of turning ch.

Rep Row 2 until panel is 30 in. (76 cm).

Ends

Work on each side of Center Section.

Row 1: With RS facing, join A in first st on right edge, ch 1, hdc in each st and ch across, turn. (122 sts)

Rows 2–4: Ch 1, working in the back horizontal bar of each hdc, hdc in each st across, turn.

Change to B.

Row 5: Ch 1, sc in first st, dc in next st, *sc in next st, dc in next st; rep from * across, turn.

Rows 6–8: Rep Row 5.

Change to C.

Row 9: Ch 1, sc in each st across, turn.

Row 10: Ch 4, sk first 2 sc, dc in next 2 sc, *ch 1, sk next sc, dc in next 2 sc; rep from * across to last 2 sts, ch 1, sk 1 st, dc in last st, turn.

Row 11: Ch 1, sc in each dc and ch-1 sp across, ending with sc in turning ch, turn.

Rows 12–17: Rep Rows 10 and 11.

Change to B.

Rows 18–21: Rep Row 5.

Change to C.

Row 22: Ch 3, (4 dc, ch 3, dc) next st, *sk next 4 sts, (4 dc, ch 3, dc) in next st; rep from * across to last 3 chs, sk next 2 chs, dc in last ch, turn.

Row 23: Ch 3, (4 dc, ch 3, dc) in each ch-3 sp across to last ch-3 sp, sk next 4 dc, dc in top of turning ch.

Fasten off.

Finishing

Add 3 in. (7.5 cm) fringe in A, B, and C in each ch-3 sp.

Weave in ends.

Baby Bobbles

Bobbles! Bobbles! Oh how I enjoy these bobbles! They are so lovely in this blanket and add the perfect touch of texture.

Yarn
Lion Brand Yarn Comfy Cotton Blend; light weight
 #3; 100% cotton; 7 oz (200 g)/392 yds (358 m)
 per skein
3 skeins: 756-098 Whipped Cream (**A**)
1 skein: 756-712 Chai Latte (**B**)

Hooks and Other Materials
US size J-10 (6 mm) crochet hook
Yarn needle

Finished Measurements
28 in. (71 cm) wide and 48 in. (122 cm) long

Gauge
14 sts x 16 rows = 4 in. (10 cm) in sc

Special Stitches
Bobble: Yo, insert hook in next st and draw up a lp,
 yo, draw through 2 lps, (yo, insert hook in next
 st and draw up a lp, yo, draw through 2 lps) 4
 times, yo and draw through all 6 lps on hook to
 complete.

Pattern Notes
- The beginning ch 3 counts as the first dc.
- The beginning ch 4 counts as the first dc plus
 ch 1.
- For photo tutorial on working into the back loop
 only (blo), see Stitch Guide on page 136.
- To change yarn color, work last st of old color
 to last yarn over. Yarn over with new color and
 draw through all loops on hook to complete st.
 Fasten off old color. Proceed with new color. (See
 photo tutorial in Stitch Guide on page 133.)

INSTRUCTIONS
With A, ch 110.
Row 1 (RS): Sc in 2nd ch from hook and in each ch
 across, turn. (109 sts)
Rows 2–36: Ch 1, sc in each st across, turn.
Change to B.
Rows 37–40: Ch 2, working in the blo, hdc in each
 st across, turn.
Change to A.
Rows 41–43: Ch 1, sc in each st across, turn.

Row 44: Ch 1, sc in next 5 sts, bobble in next st, *sc
 in next 8 sts, bobble in next st; rep from * across
 to last 4 sts, sc in last 4 sts, turn.
Rows 45–47: Ch 1, sc in each st across, turn.
Row 48: Ch 1, sc in next 10 sts, bobble, *sc in next
 8 sts, bobble in next st; rep from * across to last

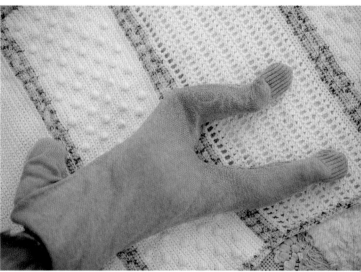

8 sts, sc in last 7 sts, 2 sc in last st, turn.

Rows 49–72: Rep Rows 41–48.

Rows 73–76: Ch 1, sc in each st across, turn.

Change to B.

Rows 77–80: Ch 2, working in the blo, hdc in each st across, turn.

Change to A.

Row 81: Ch 1, sc in each st across, turn.

Row 82: Ch 4, sk next st, dc in next st, *ch 1, sk next st, dc in next st; rep from * across, turn.

Row 83: Ch 3, *sk next ch-1 sp, dc in next st, dc in skipped ch-1 sp; rep from * across, ending last rep with dc in 3rd ch of turning ch, turn.

Row 84: Ch 4, *dc in next st, ch 1, sk next st; rep from * across, ending with dc in top of turning ch.

Rows 85–96: Rep Rows 83 and 84.

Change to B.

Rows 97–100: Ch 2, working in the blo, hdc in each st across, turn.

Change to A.

Rows 101–136: Rep Rows 41–76.

Change to B.

Rows 137–140: Ch 2, working in the blo, hdc in each st across, turn.

Change to A.

Rows 141–176: Ch 1, sc in each st across, turn.

Change to B.

Border

Rnd 1: Ch 1, turn to work along side edge, sc evenly along that edge to next corner, work 3 sc in first sc of Row 1, sc evenly across to last st, work 3 sc in last st, sc evenly along remaining edge, work 3 sc in first sc of Row 176, sc evenly across top edge to last st, work 3 sc in last st, sl st to first sc to join.

Rnd 2: Ch 1, sc in each st around with 3 sc in each corner; join with sl st to first sc. Fasten off.

Finishing

Weave in ends.

Chickadee Round Blanket

This lovely blanket is a treat to crochet. Pick a bold color, like this blue, or make it in a pretty soft pink. You'll love the look each time!

Yarn
Willow Yarns Honeybee; bulky weight #5; 69% acrylic/17% nylon/14% wool; 3.5 oz (100 g)/54 yds (49 m) per skein
7 skeins: 0007 Great Falls

Hooks and Other Materials
US size M-13 (9 mm) crochet hook
Yarn needle

Finished Measurements
34 in (86 cm) diameter

Gauge
Rnds 1–4 = 4 in. (10 cm)

Special Stitches
Double crochet 2 sts together (dc2tog): (Yo, insert hook in next st and draw up a lp, yo and draw through 2 lps) twice, yo and draw through all 3 lps on hook (1 st decreased). (See photo tutorial in Stitch Guide on page 142.)
Double crochet 3 sts together (dc3tog): (Yo, insert hook in next st and draw up a lp, yo, draw through 2 lps) 3 times, yo and draw through all 4 lps on hook (2 sts decreased). (See photo tutorial in Stitch Guide on page 143.)

Pattern Notes
- The beginning ch 3 counts as the first dc.
- The beginning ch 5 counts as the first dc plus ch 2.
- The beginning ch 6 counts as the first dc plus ch 3.

INSTRUCTIONS
Ch 5; join with a sl st to first ch to form a ring.

Rnd 1: Ch 5, (dc, ch 1) 11 times in ring; join with a sl st to 3rd ch of beg ch 5. (12 dc + 12 ch-1 sps)

Rnd 2: Ch 6, *dc in next dc, ch 3; rep from * around; join to 3rd ch of beg ch 6. (12 dc + 12 ch-3 sps)

Rnd 3: Sl st to next ch-3 sp, ch 4, 3 dc in same sp, ch 1, *4 dc in next ch-3 sp, ch 1; rep from * around; join with a sl st to beg ch 3. (48 dc + 12 ch-1 sps)

Rnd 4: Ch 5, *dc in sp between the 2nd and 3rd dc, ch 2**, dc in ch-1 sp, ch 2; rep from * around, ending last rep at **; join with a sl st in 3rd ch of beg ch 5. (24 dc + 24 ch-2 sps)

Rnd 5: Sl st in ch-2 sp, ch 3, 2 dc in same sp, ch 1, *3 dc in next ch-2 sp, ch 1; rep from * around; join with a sl st to beg ch 3. (72 dc + 24 ch-1 sps)

Rnd 6: *Ch 4, sl st in next ch-1 sp; rep from * around. (24 ch-4 sps)

Rnd 7: *Sl st in next ch-4 sp, (ch 2, sl st) 3 times in same sp; rep from * around; do not join.

Rnd 8: Sl st in first ch-2 lp, ch 2, dc2tog using next 2 ch-2 lps, ch 4, *dc3tog using next 3 ch-2 lps, ch 4; rep from * around; join with a sl st to first dc. (24 ch-4 sps + 24 dc)

Rnd 9: Ch 1, sc in same st as joining, 5 dc in next ch-4 sp, *sc in next dc, 5 dc in next ch-4 sp; rep from * around; join with a sl st to first sc. (120 dc + 24 sc)

Rnd 10: Sl st in next 2 dc, ch 1, sc in same st, *ch 3, sk 1 dc, sc in next dc, ch 3**, sk 1 dc, sk 1 sc, sk 1 dc, sc in next dc; rep from * around, ending last rep at **; join with sl st to the first sc.

Rnd 11: Sl st in sc and in next 3 chs, sl st in next sc, sl st in ch-3 sp, ch 3 (counts as dc), 3 dc in same sp, ch 3, *3 dc in next ch-sp, ch 3; rep from * around; join with sl st to beg ch 3. (24 3-dc groups + 24 ch-3 groups).

Rnd 12: Sl st in next dc, ch 1, sc in same st, 5 dc in next ch-3 sp, *sk 1 dc, sc in next dc, 5 dc in next ch-3 sp; rep from * around; join with sl st to the first st.

Rnd 13. Ch 5, dc in same st, ch 1, *sk 2 dc, sc in next dc, ch 1, sk next 2 dc, (dc, ch 3, dc) in next sc, ch 1, sk 2 dc, sc in next dc; rep from * around; join with sl st to 3rd ch of beg ch 5.

Rnd 14: Ch 3, dc in each ch and st around; join with sl st to beg ch 3.

Rnd 15: Sl st to next ch-1 sp, ch 3, sk 1 dc, *dc in next dc, ch 1, sk 1 st; rep from * around; join with sl st to beg ch 3. (84 dc + 84 ch-1 sps)

Rnd 16: Ch 3, 6 dc in same sp, sl st in next ch-1 sp, *7 dc in next ch-1 sp, sl st in next ch-1 sp; rep from * around; join with sl st to beg ch 3.

Fasten off.

Finishing
Weave in ends.

Cutie Patootie
Stitch Sampler

Stitch sampler blankets can be so colorful! With only four colors but the illusion of more, this blanket is a stunning design to crochet.

Yarn

Premier Anti-Pilling Worsted; medium weight #4; 100% acrylic; 3.5 oz (100 g)/180 yds (165 m) per skein

3 skeins each: Chinchilla (**A**), Glass (**B**), Cream (**C**), Soft Peach (**D**)

Hooks and Other Materials

US size J-10 (6 mm) crochet hook

Yarn needle

Finished Measurements

30 in. (76 cm) wide and 58 in. (147 cm) long

Gauge

14 sts x 16 rows = 4 in. (10 cm) in sc

Special Stitches

Back post slip stitch (bp sl st): Insert hook from back to front to back again, going around post of indicated st, draw up a loop and pull it all the way through the loop on the hook as for a sl st.

Pattern Notes

- The beginning ch 2 will not count as a st.
- The beginning ch 3 counts as the first dc.
- The beginning ch 4 counts as the first dc plus ch 1.
- To change yarn color, work last st of old color to last yarn over. Yarn over with new color and draw through all loops on hook to complete st. Fasten off old color. Proceed with new color. (See photo tutorial in Stitch Guide on page 133.)

INSTRUCTIONS

With A, ch 84.

Row 1: Sc in 2nd ch and in each ch across, turn. (83 sc)

Row 2: Ch 4, sk 1 st, dc in next st, *ch 1, sk 1 st, dc in next st; rep from * across, turn.

Row 3: Ch 1, sc in first dc, * sc in ch-1 sp, sc in next dc; rep from * across, turn.

Change to B.

Row 4: Ch 1, hdc in each st across, turn.

Change to C.

Row 5: Ch 2, dc in each st across, turn.

Change to D.

Row 6: Ch 1, sc in first dc, bp sl st across to last st, sc in last st, turn.

Change to C.

Row 7: Using sts from Row 5, ch 2, dc in each st across, turn.

Change to A.

Row 8: Ch 1, sc in first 2 dc, *ch 2, sk 2 sts, sc in next st; rep from * across, turn.

Change to B.

Row 9: Ch 3, *3 dc in ch-2 sp, ch 1, sk 1 sc; rep from * across, ending with dc in last st, turn.

Change to A.

Row 10: Ch 1, sc in first dc, sc in next ch-1 sp, *ch 2, sk 3 dc, sc in next ch-1 sp; rep from * across, ending with sc in turning ch 3, turn.

Change to C.

Row 11: Rep Row 9.

Change to A.

Row 12: Rep Row 10.

Change to D.

Row 13: Rep Row 9.

Change to A.

Row 14: Rep Row 10.

Change to C.

Row 15: Ch 1, sc in first sc, *2 sc in ch-2 sp, sc in next sc; rep from * across to last st, sc in last st, turn.

Row 16: Ch 1, sc in each st across, turn.

Change to D.

Row 17: Ch 3, dc in same st, sk 1 st, *2 dc in next st, sk 1 st; rep from * across, ending with dc in last st, turn.

Change to A.

Row 18: Rep Row 15.

Change to C.

Row 19: Ch 1, sc in each st across, turn.

Change to B.

Row 20: Ch 1, sc in first st, *dc in next st, sc in next st; rep from * across, turn.

Change to D.

Row 21: Ch 3, *sc in next st, dc in next st; rep from * across, turn.

Change to B.

Row 22: Rep Row 20.

Change to D.

Row 23: Rep Row 21.

Change to A.

Rows 24–89: Rep Rows 2–23 3 times.

Border

Rnd 1: With A, ch 3, 2 dc in same st, turn to work along side edge, dc evenly along edge to next corner, work 3 dc in first st of Row 1, dc evenly across to last st, work 3 dc in last st, dc evenly along remaining edge, work 3 dc in first st of Row 99, dc evenly across top edge to last st; join with sl st to beg ch 3.

Change to C.

Rnd 2: Ch 1, sc in each st around with 3 sc in 2nd dc in each corner; join with sl st to first sc.

Change to A.

Rnd 3: Ch 3, dc in each st around with 3 dc in 2nd sc in each corner; join with sl st to beg ch 3.

Fasten off.

Finishing

Weave in ends.

Half Pint Blanket

Wrap your baby in color and warmth with this fun stitch sampler!

Yarn

Universal Yarn Deluxe Worsted Superwash; medium weight #4; 100% superwash wool; 3.5 oz (100 g)/218 yds (199 m) per skein

2 skeins each: 714 Petrol Blue (**A**), 708 Butter (**B**), 728 Pulp (**C**), 709 Lime Tree (**D**)

Hooks and Other Materials

US size I-9 (5.5 mm) crochet hook
Yarn needle

Finished Measurements

30 in. (76 cm) wide and 48 in. (122 cm) long

Gauge

14 sts x 16 rows = 4 in. (10 cm) in sc

Pattern Notes

- The beginning ch 3 counts as the first dc.
- The beginning ch 4 counts as the first dc plus ch 1.
- To change yarn color, work last st of old color to last yarn over. Yarn over with new color and draw through all loops on hook to complete st. Fasten off old color. Proceed with new color. (See photo tutorial in Stitch Guide on page 133.)
- The blanket is made in two sections. Section 1 is the vertical section and Section 2 will be made horizontally on the edge of Section 1.

INSTRUCTIONS

Section 1 (Vertical)

With A, ch 129.

Row 1 (RS): Sc in 2nd ch from hook and in each ch across, turn. (128 sc)

Row 2: Ch 1, sc in each st across, turn.

Change to B.

Row 3: Ch 3, sk first sc, dc in next st, *ch 2, sk next 2 sts, dc in next 2 sts; rep from * across, turn.

Row 4: Ch 4, 2 dc in next ch-2 sp, (ch 2, 2 dc) in each ch-2 sp across to last ch-sp, ch 1, sk next dc, dc in 3rd ch of turning ch, turn.

Change to C.

Row 5: Ch 1, sc in first dc, sc in next ch-1 sp, sc in next 2 dc, *2 sc in next ch-2 sp, sc in next 2 dc; rep from * across to last ch-1 sp, sc in ch-1 sp, sc in 3rd ch of turning ch, turn.

Row 6: Ch 1, sc in each st across, turn.

Change to D.

Rows 7 and 8: Rep Rows 3 and 4.

Change to A.

Rows 9 and 10: Rep Rows 5 and 6.

Change to B.

Rows 11 and 12: Rep Rows 3 and 4.

Change to C.

Rows 13 and 14: Rep Rows 5 and 6.

Change to D.
Rows 15–70: Rep Rows 7–14.
Fasten off.

Section 2 (Horizontal)

Row 1: With RS facing, join D in top right stitch,
 work along side edge, sc 110 across evenly, turn.
Row 2: Ch 3 (first dc), *dc in next 2 sts, ch 2, sk 2,
 rep from * across, ending with 1 dc in last st,
 turn.
Row 3: Ch 1, sc in each st and 2 sc in each ch-2 sp,
 turn.
Rows 4–26: Rep Rows 2 and 3, ending on Row 2.
Change to C.
Rows 27 and 28: Rep Rows 2 and 3.
Change to A.
Rows 29–37: Rep Row 2 and 3, ending on Row 2.
Fasten off.

Finishing

Weave in ends.

Wiggle-Worm Blanket

Learn a few new stitches with this dazzling stitch sampler. Utilize the front and back post stitches to create texture!

Yarn

Cascade Yarns Cherub Chunky; medium weight #5; 55% nylon/45% acrylic; 3.5 oz (100 g)/136.7 yds (125 m) per skein

4 skeins each: 08 Baby Blue (**A**), 35 Taupe (**B**), 01 White (**C**)

5 skeins: 58 Blue Shadow (**D**)

Hooks and Other Materials

US size J-10 (6 mm) crochet hook
Yarn needle

Finished Measurements

30 in. (76 cm) wide and 52 in. (132 cm) long

Gauge

14 sts x 16 rows = 4 in. (10 cm) in sc

Special Stitches

Back Post Double Crochet (BPdc): Yo, insert hook from back to front then to back, going around post of indicated st, draw up a loop, (yo and draw through 2 loops on hook) twice. Skip st in front of the BPdc. (See photo tutorial in Stitch Guide on page 145.)

Front Post Double Crochet (FPdc): Yo, insert hook from front to back then to front, going around post of indicated st, draw up a loop, (yo and draw through 2 loops on hook) twice. Skip st behind the FPdc. (See photo tutorial in Stitch Guide on page 144.)

Front Post Treble Crochet (FPtr): Yo twice, insert hook from front to back then to front, going around post of indicated st, draw a loop around the post, (yo and draw through 2 loops on hook) 3 times. Skip st behind the FPtr. (See photo tutorial in Stitch Guide on page 146.)

Front Post Treble Crochet 2 sts Together (FPtr-2tog): Yo twice, insert hook from front to back then to front, going around post of next st, yo and draw up a loop, (yo and draw through 2 loops on hook) 2 times; yo twice, insert hook from front to back then to front, going around post of next st, yo and draw up a loop, (yo and draw through 2 loops on hook) 2 times; yo and draw through all loops on hook. (See photo tutorial in Stitch Guide on pages 148–149.)

Hdc in back horizontal bar: Locate the *top* loops you normally crochet into. On the WS (or back side) of the hdc, you'll see a horizontal bar. Work your hdc into this bar. (See photo tutorial in Stitch Guide on page 139.)

Pattern Notes

- The beginning ch 2 will not count as a st unless otherwise stated.
- The beginning ch 3 counts as the first dc.

- For photo tutorial on working into the back loop only (blo), see Stitch Guide on page 136.
- To change yarn color, work last st of old color to last yarn over. Yarn over with new color and draw through all loops on hook to complete st. Fasten off old color. Proceed with new color. (See photo tutorial in Stitch Guide on page 133.)

INSTRUCTIONS

With A, ch 111.

Row 1 (RS): Hdc in 2nd ch from hook and in each across, turn. (110 sts)

Row 2: Ch 2, working in the back horizontal bar of each hdc, hdc in each st across, turn.

Row 3: Ch 2, working in blo, hdc in each st across, turn.

Row 4: Rep Row 2.

Change to B.

Row 5: Ch 3, working in blo, dc in each st, turn.

Row 6: Ch 3, FPdc on next 4 sts, BPdc on next 5 sts, *FPdc on next 5 sts, BPdc on next 5 sts; rep from * across, turn.

Rows 7 and 8: Rep Row 6.

Row 9: Ch 3, BPdc on next 4 sts, FPdc on next 5 sts, *BPdc on next 5 sts, BPdc on next 5 sts; rep from *across, turn.

Rows 10 and 11: Rep Row 9.

Change to C.

Row 12: Ch 2, hdc in each st across, turn.

Row 13: Ch 2, working in the blo, hdc in each st across, turn.

Row 14: Ch 2, working in back horizontal bar of each hdc, hdc in each st across, turn.

Change to D.

Row 15: Ch 1, working in the blo, sc in each st across, turn.

Row 16: Ch 3, FPdc on next st, *BPdc on next st, FPdc on next st; rep from * across, turn.

Row 17: Ch 1, sc in each st across, turn.

Row 18: Ch 1, sc in first st using the post 2 rows below, FPdc on next post, *BPdc on next post, FPdc on next post; rep from * across, turn.

Rows 19–25: Rep Rows 17 and 18, ending on Row 17.

Change to B.

Rows 26–28: Rep Rows 12–14.

Change to A.

Row 29: Ch 1, working in the blo, sc in each st across, turn.

Row 30: Ch 1, sc in each st across, turn.

Row 31: Ch 1, sc in next 7 sts, FPtr on 10th post 2 rows below, *sc in next 3 sts, FPtr on same st post as previous FPtr 2 rows below, sc in next 4 sts, sk 8 sts 2 rows below, FPtr on next post; rep from * across to last 7 sts, sc in last 7 sts, turn.

Row 32: Ch 1, sc in each st across, turn.

Row 33: Ch 1, sc in next 9 sts, FPtr2tog using the next 2 FPtr 2 rows below, *sc in next 8 sts, FPtr2tog using the next 2 FPtr 2 rows below; rep from * across to last 9 sts, sc in last 9 sts, turn.

Row 34: Ch 1, sc in each st across, turn.

Row 35: Ch 1, sc in next 7 sts, FPtr on FPtr 2 rows below, *sc in next 3 sts, FPtr on FPtr 2 rows below, sc in next 4 sts, sk 8 sts 2 rows below, FPtr on next FPtr 2 rows below, rep from * across to last 7 sts, sc in last 7 sts, turn.

Row 36: Ch 1, sc in each st across, turn.

Row 37: Rep Row 33.

Change to D.

Rows 38–40: Rep Rows 12–14.

Change to C.

Row 41: Ch 3, working in the blo, dc in each st across, turn.

Row 42: Ch 3, dc in next 2 sts, FPdc in next 2 sts, *dc in next st, FPdc in next 2 sts; rep from * across to last st, dc in last st, turn.

Row 43: Ch 3, dc in next 2 sts, FPdc on next st, *dc in next 2 sts, FPdc on next st; rep from * across, dc in last st, turn.

Rows 44–47: Rep Rows 42 and 43.

Change to A.

Rows 48–50: Rep Rows 12–14.

Rows 51–142: Rep Rows 5–50 2 times.

Fasten off.

Border

Rnd 1: With RS facing, join D in last st on left side, ch 1, turn to work along side edge, sc evenly to next corner, work 3 sc in first sc of Row 1, sc evenly across to last st, work 3 sc in last st, sc evenly along remaining edge, work 3 sc in first sc of Row 142, sc evenly across top edge to last st, work 3 sc in last st, sl st to first sc to join.

Rnd 2: Ch 1, sc in each st around with 3 sc in the 2nd sc of each corner; join with a sl st to first sc.

Fasten off.

Finishing

Weave in ends.

How to Read the Patterns

SKILL LEVELS

Beginner: Projects for first-time crocheters using basic stitches. Minimal shaping.

Easy: Projects with basic stitches, repetitive stitch patterns, simple color changes, and simple shaping and finishing.

Intermediate: Projects using a variety of techniques, such as basic lace patterns or color patterns, mid-level shaping, and finishing.

Experienced: Projects with intricate stitch patterns, techniques, and dimensions, such as nonrepeating patterns, multicolor techniques, fine threads, small hooks, detailed shaping, and refined finishing.

YARN

You will find listed the specific yarn(s) and colors I used to crochet the pattern, plus how many skeins you'll need. Also included is that specific yarn's "yarn weight." You'll find this information on the label of every skein of yarn you buy, and it ranges from #0 lace weight to #7 jumbo weight. If you can't find the specific yarn I use or you'd like to use something else, knowing the yarn weight will let you pick another yarn that will have the same gauge.

HOOKS AND OTHER MATERIALS

Each pattern will list the crochet hook recommended for that project. Always start with the size hook stated and check the gauge before starting the project. Change the hook size as necessary to obtain the correct gauge so that the project will be finished in the correct size.

Items you will need to complete the patterns in this book include crochet hooks, scissors, stitch markers, yarn, ruler, and a yarn needle for weaving in ends or sewing pieces together.

Standard Yarn Weight System

Categories of yarn, gauge ranges, and recommended needle and hook sizes

Yarn Weight Symbol & Category Names	**0** LACE	**1** SUPER FINE	**2** FINE	**3** LIGHT	**4** MEDIUM	**5** BULKY	**6** SUPER BULKY	**7** JUMBO
Type of Yarns in Category	Fingering, 10-Count Crochet Thread	Sock, Fingering, Baby	Sport, Baby	DK, Light Worsted	Worsted, Afghan, Aran	Chunky, Craft, Rug	Bulky, Roving	Jumbo, Roving
Knit Gauge Range in Stockinette Stitch to 4 inches*	33–40 sts**	27–32 sts	23–26 sts	21–24 sts	16–20 sts	12–15 sts	7–11 sts	6 sts and fewer
Recommended Needle in Metric Size Range	1.5–2.25 mm	2.25–3.25 mm	3.25–3.75 mm	3.75–4.5 mm	4.5–5.5 mm	5.5–8 mm	8–12.75 mm	12.75 mm and larger
Recommended Needle in U.S. Size Range	000 to 1	1 to 3	3 to 5	5 to 7	7 to 9	9 to 11	11 to 17	17 and larger
Crochet Gauge Ranges in Single Crochet to 4 inches*	32–42 double crochets**	21–32 sts	16–20 sts	12–17 sts	11–14 sts	8–11 sts	7–9 sts	6 sts and fewer
Recommended Hook in Metric Size Range	Steel*** 1.6–1.4 mm Regular hook 2.25 mm	2.25–3.5 mm	3.5–4.5 mm	4.5–5.5 mm	5.5–6.5 mm	6.5–9 mm	9–15 mm	15 mm and larger
Recommended Hook in U.S. Size Range	Steel 6, 7, 8*** Regular hook B–1	B–1 to E–4	E–4 to 7	7 to I–9	I–9 to K–10½	K–10½ to M–13	M–13 to Q	Q and larger

* GUIDELINES ONLY: The above reflect the most commonly used gauges and needle or hook sizes for specific yarn categories.

** Lace weight yarns are usually knitted or crocheted on larger needles and hooks to create lacy, openwork patterns. Accordingly, a gauge range is difficult to determine. Always follow the gauge stated in your pattern.

*** Steel crochet hooks are sized differently from regular hooks—the higher the number, the smaller the hook, which is the reverse of regular hook sizing.

*Source: Craft Yarn Council of America's **www.YarnStandards.com**

GAUGE

Exact gauge is essential for proper size. Before beginning your project, make a sample swatch in the stitches indicated for the gauge sample, in the yarn and hook specified. After completing the swatch, measure it, counting your stitches and rows carefully. If your swatch is larger or smaller than specified, make another, changing hook size to get the correct gauge. Keep trying until you find the size hook that will give you the specified gauge.

NOTES ON THE INSTRUCTIONS

- When a number appears before the stitch name, such as 3 dc, work these stitches into the same stitch, for example "3 dc into the next st."
- When only one stitch is to be worked into each of a number of stitches, it can be written like this, for example, "1 sc in each of next 3 sts." When a number appears after a chain, for example, ch 10, this means work the number of chains indicated.

- The asterisks mark a specific set of instructions that are repeated; for example, " * 2 sc in next st, 1 dc in next st, rep from * across," means repeat the stitches from the asterisk to next given instruction.
- When instructions are given within parentheses, it can mean three things. For example, "(2 dc, ch 1, 2 dc) in the next st" means work 2 dc, ch 1, 2 dc all into the same stitch. It can also mean a set of stitches repeated a number of times, for example "(sc in next st, 2 sc in next st) 6 times." Last, the number(s) given in parentheses at the end of a row or round denote(s) the number of stitches or spaces you should have on that row or round.
- A few of the patterns include stitch instructions, which you'll find under Special Stitches. In most cases, these stitches are particular to that specific pattern.
- Be sure to read the Pattern Notes section before beginning a project. You'll find helpful hints there, and the notes will often clear up any questions you may have about the project.

Abbreviations

beg	begin/begins/beginning
blo	back loop only
BPdc	back post double crochet
BPsc	back post single crochet
BPtr	back post treble crochet
ch(s)	chain/chains
ch-sp(s)	chain spaces(s)
cl(s)	cluster(s)
cm	centimeters
dc	double crochet
dc2tog	double crochet 2 stitches together
dc3tog	double crochet 3 stitches together
dec	decrease
flo	front loop only
FPdc	front post double crochet
FPsc	front post single crochet
FPtr	front post treble crochet
g	gram(s)
hdc	half double crochet
hdc2tog	half double crochet 2 stitches together
in.	inch(es)
inc	increase
lp(s)	loop(s)
mm	millimeter
oz	ounce(s)
rem	remaining
rep(s)	repeat(s)
rnd(s)	round(s)
RS	right side
sc	single crochet
sc2tog	single crochet 2 stitches together
sk	skip
sl st(s)	slip stitch(es)
sp(s)	space(s)
st(s)	stitch(es)
tog	together
tr	treble
tr2tog	treble crochet 2 stitches together
WS	wrong side
yd(s)	yard(s)
yo	yarn over

SYMBOLS AND TERMS

* Work instructions following * as many more times as indicated in addition to the first time.

( ) or [ ] Work enclosed instructions as many times as specified by the number immediately following or work all enclosed instructions in the stitch or space indicated or contains explanatory remarks.

Parentheses ( ) at end of row/round The number(s) given at the end of a row or round in the parentheses denote(s) the number of stitches or spaces you should have when that row or round is completed.

Stitch Guide

HOW TO HOLD YOUR HOOK

There are different ways that you can hold your hook, but I want to show you two of the most common. Try both and use the one that feels most comfortable.

Knife Hold

Hold the hook in your hand like you would a knife. Your hand is over the hook, using your thumb and middle finger to control the hook while the pointer finger is on top guiding the yarn.

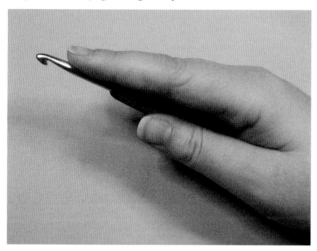

Pencil Hold

Hold the hook like you would a pencil. The hook is cradled in your hand resting on your middle finger.

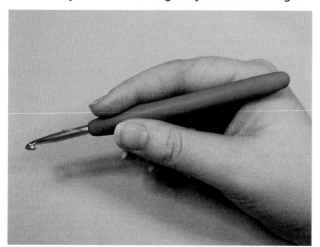

CHANGING COLORS

When changing colors, use this technique.

1. Complete your given stitch until the last pull through.

2. Yarn over the next color and pull through to finish the stitch and color change. Cut or drop the yarn from the original color.

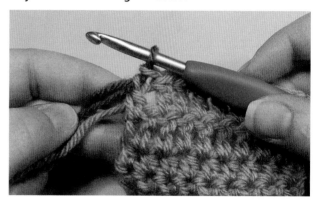

3. Continue working with joined color.

SLIPKNOT

This adjustable knot will begin every crochet project.

1. Make a loop in the yarn.

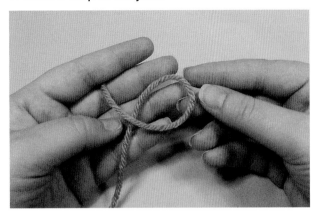

2. With crochet hook or finger, grab the yarn from the skein and pull through loop.

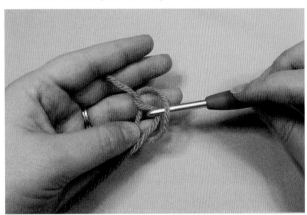

3. Pull tight on the yarn and adjust to create the first loop.

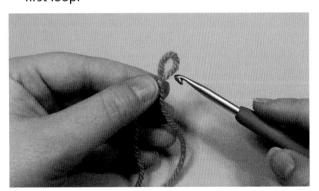

CHAIN (CH)

The chain provides the foundation for your stitches at the beginning of a pattern. It can also serve as a stitch within a pattern and can be used to create an open effect.

1. Insert hook through the slipknot and place the yarn over the hook by passing the hook in front of the yarn.

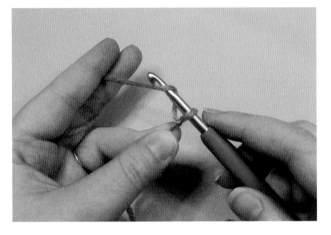

2. Keeping the yarn taut (but not too tight) pull the hook back through the loop with the yarn. Ch 1 is complete.

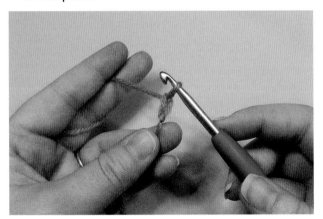

3. Repeat Steps 1 and 2 to create multiple chains.

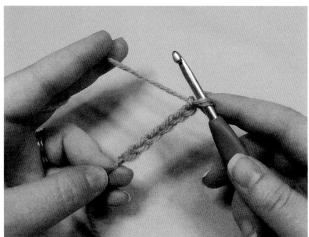

SINGLE CROCHET (SC)

1. Insert hook from the front of the stitch to the back and yarn over.

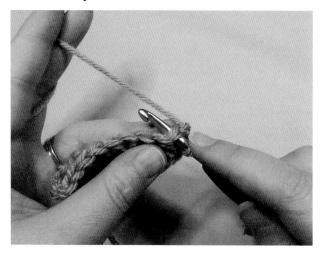

2. Pull the yarn back through the stitch: 2 loops on hook.

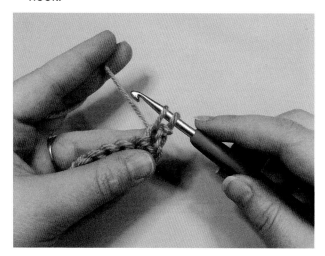

3. Yarn over and draw through both loops on the hook to complete.

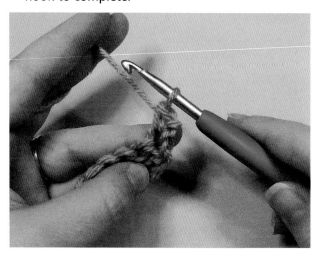

BACK LOOP AND FRONT LOOP

At times you will be instructed to work in the front loop only (flo) or the back loop only (blo) of a stitch to create a texture within the pattern.

Inserting hook to crochet into the front loop only (flo) of a stitch.

Inserting hook to crochet into the back loop only (blo) of a stitch.

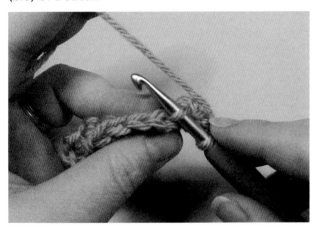

Unless specified otherwise, you will insert your hook under both loops to crochet any stitch.

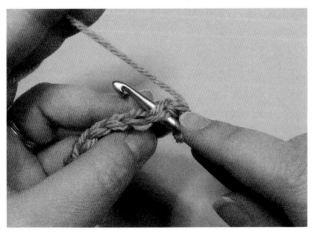

SLIP STITCH (SL ST)

The slip stitch is used to join one stitch to another or to join a stitch to another point. It can also be used within the pattern as a stitch without height.

1. Insert the hook from the front of the stitch to the back of stitch and yarn over.

2. Pull the yarn back through the stitch: 2 loops on hook.

3. Continue to pull the loop through the first loop on the hook to finish.

HALF DOUBLE CROCHET (HDC)

1. Yarn over from back to front over hook.

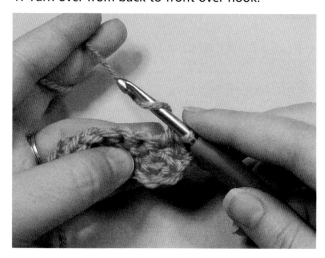

2. Insert hook from the front of the stitch to the back.

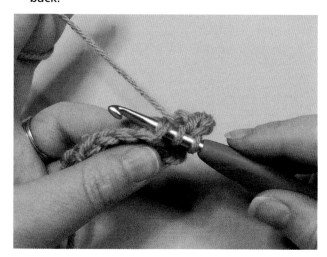

3. Yarn over and pull yarn back through stitch: 3 loops on hook.

4. Yarn over and draw through all 3 loops on hook to complete.

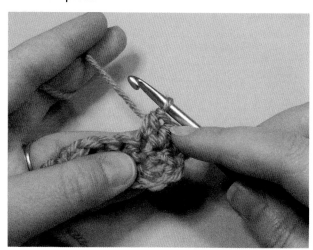

HALF DOUBLE CROCHET IN BACK HORIZONTAL BAR

1. Locate the *top* loops you normally crochet into.

3. Work into this bar as you would a stitch.

2. On the WS (or back side) of the hdc, you'll see a horizontal bar.

DOUBLE CROCHET (DC)

1. Yarn over and insert the hook from the front of the stitch to the back.

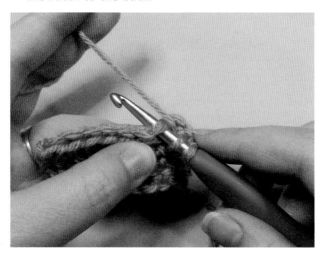

2. Yarn over and pull the yarn back through the stitch: 3 loops on hook.

3. Yarn over and draw the yarn through the first 2 loops on the hook: 2 loops on hook.

4. Yarn over and draw the yarn through the last 2 loops on hook to complete.

TREBLE CROCHET (TR)

1. Yarn over 2 times.

2. Insert the hook from the front of the stitch to the back. Yarn over and pull the yarn back through the stitch: 4 loops on hook.

3. To complete: (Yarn over and draw the yarn through the first 2 loops on the hook) 3 times.

SINGLE CROCHET 2 TOGETHER (SC2TOG)

A single crochet 2 together (also known as a decrease) will take two stitches and make them into one single crochet stitch.

1. Insert the hook from the front of the stitch to the back and yarn over. Pull the yarn back through the stitch: 2 loops on hook.

2. Leaving the loops on the hook, insert the hook front to back in the next stitch. Yarn over and pull back through stitch: 3 loops on hook.

3. Yarn over and draw through all 3 loops on the hook to complete.

DOUBLE CROCHET 2 TOGETHER (DC2TOG)

A double crochet 2 together will take two stitches and make them into one double crochet stitch.

1. Yarn over and insert the hook from the front of the stitch to the back. Yarn over and pull the yarn back through the stitch: 3 loops on hook.

2. Yarn over and draw the yarn through the first 2 loops on the hook: 2 loops on hook.

3. Leaving the loops on the hook, yarn over and insert the hook from front to back into the next stitch. Yarn over and pull back through the stitch: 4 loops on hook.

4. Yarn over and draw the yarn through the first 2 loops on the hook: 3 loops on hook.

5. Yarn over and draw the yarn through all 3 loops on hook to complete.

DOUBLE CROCHET 3 TOGETHER (DC3TOG)

A double crochet 3 together will take three stitches and make them into one double crochet stitch.

1. Yarn over and insert the hook from the front of the stitch to the back. Yarn over and pull the yarn back through the stitch: 3 loops on hook.

2. Yarn over and draw the yarn through the first 2 loops on the hook: 2 loops on hook.

3. Leaving the loops on the hook, yarn over and insert the hook from front to back into the next stitch. Yarn over and pull back through the stitch (as shown in photo), yarn over and draw the yarn through the first 2 loops on the hook: 3 loops on hook.

4. Leaving the loops on the hook, yarn over and insert the hook from front to back into the next stitch. Yarn over and pull back through the stitch: 5 loops on hook.

5. Yarn over and draw the yarn through the first 2 loops on the hook: 4 loops on hook.

6. Yarn over and draw the yarn through all 4 loops on hook to complete.

POST STITCHES

Each stitch has a post. When working a front post stitch or back post stitch, work around the post instead of into the top of the stitch.

This is the post of a double crochet.

Front Post Double Crochet (FPdc)

1. Yarn over and insert the hook from the front to the back to the front around the post of the stitch.

2. Yarn over and pull the yarn back around the post: 3 loops on the hook.

3. Complete like a double crochet: Yarn over and draw the yarn through the first 2 loops on the hook: 2 loops remain on the hook. Yarn over and draw the yarn through the last 2 loops on the hook to complete.

Back Post Double Crochet (BPdc)

1. To work the back post double crochet simply work from back to front to back around the post and complete Steps 2 and 3 as for the front post double crochet.

2. Yarn over and pull the yarn back around the post: 3 loops on the hook.

3. Complete like a double crochet: Yarn over and draw the yarn through the first 2 loops on the hook: 2 loops remain on the hook. Yarn over and draw the yarn through the last 2 loops on the hook to complete.

Front Post Treble Crochet (FPtr)

1. Yarn over twice, insert hook from front to back to the front around the post of the stitch.

2. Yarn over and pull the yarn back around the post: 4 loops on hook.

3. (Yarn over and draw through 2 loops on hook) 3 times.

Back Post Treble Crochet (BPtr)

1. To work the back post treble crochet yarn over twice and work from back to front to back around the post and complete Steps 2 and 3 as for front post treble crochet.

2. Yarn over and pull the yarn back around the post: 4 loops on hook.

3. (Yarn over and draw through 2 loops on hook) 3 times.

Front Post Treble Crochet 2 Together (FPtr2tog)

1. Yarn over twice, insert hook from front to back then to front, going around post of next stitch, draw up a loop: 4 loops on hook.

3. Yarn over twice, insert hook from front to back then to front, going around post of next stitch, draw up a loop: 5 loops on hook.

2. (Yarn over and draw through 2 loops on hook) 2 times: 2 loops remain on hook.

4. (Yo and draw through 2 loops on hook) 2 times: 3 loops on hook.

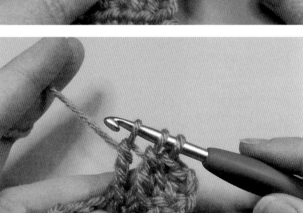

5. Yarn over and draw through all 3 loops on hook.

REVERSE SINGLE CROCHET (REV SC)
Single crochet worked from left to right (right to left, if left-handed).

1. Insert hook into next stitch to the right (left), under loop on hook, and draw up a loop.

2. Yarn over, draw through all loops on hook.

Acknowledgments

First and foremost, thank you to Jason, my wonderful husband. You are my biggest fan and supporter! Thank you for being in my corner no matter what comes our way! To our children, we love you and you are our world!

A huge thanks to Candi Derr and the Stackpole team. Thanks for your support throughout this blanket adventure!

To all of the yarn companies, your support is very much appreciated! Your yarns have made this book shine and I couldn't do it without you!

To my lead stitch assistant, Tabatha Widner, and my other stitch assistants, Clara Bushnell and Victoria Tutwiler. Your testing and help are appreciated more than you know!

And last but not least, a huge thanks to Heather Alvarado, owner of Heartstrings Photography, and all of the parents with the cutest babies. The photography and babies have brought life to these blankets!

Visual Index

Sweet Pea Blanket   2

Woven Love Stroller
Blanket   6

Franklin Drake
Blanket   10

Candy Lane
Blankie   14

Sunny Days
Blanket   18

Baby Delight   22

Cocoa Strips   26

Cupcake Squares
Blanket   30

Canterbury Bells   34

Low Tide Motif
Blanket   38

Snuggle-Buggle Baby
Blanket   44

Blueberry Bliss   52

Rosebud Blanket   54

Triangle Angel
Blanket   58

Cutiekins Blanket   62

Speckled Blanket   66

Cuddle and Play   70

Sherbet Squares   74

Honeydew
Blanket   78

Asher Log Cabin   82

Rock-a-Bye-Baby
Blanket   88

Blossom Motif Baby
Blanket   92

Cloudberry   98

Happy Time   102

Ethelyn Dreams
Blankie   106

Baby Bobbles   110

Chickadee Round
Blanket   114

Cutie Patootie Stitch
Sampler   118

Half Pint
Blanket   122

Wiggle-Worm
Blanket   126